A CANADIAN QUILT

Stories of Immigrants

SHRINIVAS SAWANT

ISBN
Paperback 979-8-89724-934-3
Hardcase 979-8-89906-273-5

Dedication

This book is lovingly dedicated to my cherished parents: my mother, Laxmi Sawant; my father, Mahadeo Sawant; my aunt, Rajani Sawant; and my uncle, Pandurang Sawant. Their unwavering support, love, and guidance have shaped me into the person I am today. They instilled in me a sense of purpose and inspired me to strive for excellence in every facet of life. Their blessings and enduring presence, even beyond this earthly realm, continue to be a source of strength, courage, and motivation, enabling me to embrace new challenges and explore uncharted territories. This book is a heartfelt expression of my eternal love and gratitude for them.

My journey began in the serene village of Kalsuli, nestled in the Sindhudurga District of the Konkan region in India, where I was born in the 1970s. My formative years were spent in this tranquil setting, where I completed my schooling before moving to Mumbai in 1983 as a teenager. Mumbai became the canvas of my aspirations, where I pursued my education, built my career, got married, and established my own home. This vibrant city also served as the Launchpad for my professional journeys across various countries.

In 2013, I embarked on a new chapter, moving to Canada in search of better opportunities. My time there was transformative, filled with valuable experiences and personal growth. By the end of 2016, I returned to India, enriched with insights and memories that inspired me to document my journey and share my learnings through writing.

This book is also dedicated to all the incredible individuals I encountered along the way — friends, colleagues, and kindred spirits — whose influence and kindness have left an indelible mark on my life. To each of you who touched my journey, this book is a tribute to your presence and the role you played in shaping my story.

Contents

Authors Note

I am thrilled to present this book, "A Canadian Quilt — Stories of Immigrants." This marks my second book in English and my fifth authored work overall. It is inspired by my fourth book, originally published in Marathi in December 2023, which received an great response from readers. I am currently working on the second edition of my Marathi Book while simultaneously bringing this English version to fruition.

My journey as an author began in 2020, during the global lockdown. Faced with home confinement and solitude, I sought solace in storytelling and embarked on conducting online interviews titled "Volunteers in Action." These interactions, coupled with my "My Story: Adapting to the New Normal" series, ignited my passion for writing. Subsequently, I ventured into filmmaking to highlight the plight of sanitation workers, further deepening my commitment to social storytelling. Drawing from my training materials and simplifying complex subjects, I crafted my first book, published in 2023, which was warmly received and set me on my journey as an author.

This book is a heartfelt compilation of stories about the incredible individuals I encountered along the way. Each narrative is a thread in the rich tapestry of immigrant experiences, woven together with care and respect.

I owe a debt of gratitude to my wife, Sailee Sawant, whose unwavering support and constructive critiques have been my anchor throughout this journey. Her encouragement has kept me focused and driven. I am thankful to my Brother and Mentor Dr. Umeshchandra Sawant, My Sister in Law Priyadarshini Sawant, All my brothers and cousins and entire Sawant family for their encouragements and support to me. I extend my heartfelt thanks to Dr. Shital Gosavi, who skillfully translated my Marathi book, "Ashritancha Desh," into English, providing a first draft that I could build upon and refine it further.

I am deeply thankful to Mr. Arno Ilic, my mentor and friend from Canada, as well as Ms. Yamini Surenkumar and Ms. Manisha Sawant, for their invaluable feedback and suggestions during the proofreading process. Their insights have significantly enhanced the quality of this book. My sincere thanks also go to Mr. Jagdish Chanrai and Sunder Chanrai for their support and constant encouragement and motivation to see this project through to completion. Lastly, I express my gratitude to" Notion Press Publishing" who masterfully designed the cover and handled the typesetting of this book.

Thank you for accompanying me on this journey of stories and experiences. I hope this book resonates with you as deeply as these stories have touched my life.

Shrinivas Sawant

Introduction

"A Canadian Quilt - "Stories of Immigrants" presents the unique stories of selected individuals I met and my real experiences while living in Canada these stories are neither entirely true nor entirely false. As I saw those people, I saw myself reflected in them; their stories are not theirs alone, but also mine. The depiction of those individuals might have been accurate or not; perhaps they were. Perhaps you will recognize them, and it will only be a coincidence. These individuals, who create an environment around us, can be found in any country worldwide. Somewhere, as a writer, I have taken the liberty to narrate their stories. This story is not about their victories or defeats but their life struggles. The decision to go to another country, the struggle to make a living there, the conflict they face with their own lives, and the solutions they find are the subjects of this book.

I spent four years in Canada trying to live a different life and make my career, during which I came into contact with hundreds of people. I made new friends and learned new things. I learned a lot from the social and political systems of Canada. I also started exploring new things about myself. I discovered new meanings of joy, happiness, contentment, success, and failure. Amidst the effort to establish my existence, I kept meeting people who seemed to be struggling with their own lives, and through their struggles I found my path but never felt the need to criticize the institutions, government, individuals, or social systems there. Instead, I underwent significant changes within myself and in my perception by staying alongside those changed social systems. During my stay in Canada I met many people there. In my own struggle of settling in Canada I witness there struggles as well. I have written about them in my diary. For this Book, I have selected only 13 stories from my diary as all stories do not relate directly to my career struggle there, that's why the other stories couldn't find a place in this book. I hope readers will enjoy this stories and this book.

Thank you,

Shrinivas Sawant

रहना नहिं देस बिराना है।

यह संसार कागद की पुड़िया, बूँद पड़े घुल जाना है।

यह संसार काँट की बाड़ी, उलझपुलझ- मरि जाना है।

यह संसार झाड़ औ झाँखर, आग लगे बरि जाना है।

कहत कबीर सुनो भाई साधो, सतगुरु नाम ठिकाना है॥

संत कबीर

To stay is not easy; this world is transient.

It's like a paper boat, destined to dissolve with a drop.

This world is like a thorny bush, entangled and eventually perishing.

This world is like a tree in a storm, destined to be consumed by fire.

Says Kabir, listen, O brothers and seekers, the true abode is in the name of the Satguru.

Sant Kabir

The Journey Abroad

Chapter One

The Journey Abroad

> " A journey of a thousand miles begins with a single step."

– Lao Tzu

Leaving one's homeland for a better future is a story we often hear in ancient tales and modern autobiographies. Many have set out, hoping to build a better life and searching for new chances. Sometimes, these journeys are filled with joy; sometimes, they bring challenges. But at the center of it all is a simple wish—to find success and start fresh. For many of us, this dream is planted in our minds from a young age.

My journey abroad started with business trips, not with plans of settling. Travelling as a tourist or for work meetings differs significantly from living in a place. When you are a visitor, everything feels new and exciting. You visit markets, malls, and famous spots and meet people from different walks of life. But when you decide to make that place your home, that's when the real challenges begin.

In 2002, I made my first trip outside India, spending two weeks in Great Britain for office meetings. London was my first taste of life outside of India, and it was an eye-opener. Between meetings, I explored the city—its famous landmarks, clean streets, and mix of cultures. London's cool climate and quiet order were a complete change from the heat and liveliness of India.

Each year after that, our meetings were held in London, and every visit made me more curious about the city. In 2004, one of my colleagues got a job in London, and I became even more interested in what life there might be like. Over the next few years, I travelled to many places—Dubai, Thailand, Argentina, Brazil, Nepal, Bangladesh, Canada, and the United States. Every country was unique, with its own culture and way of life.

 To travel is to take a journey into yourself."

– Danny Kaye

Then, in 2010, I took a bigger step. For personal reasons, I decided to settle abroad and chose Canada. Within six months, I received permanent residency, and in April 2013, I left India and moved to Toronto. Securing a skilled visa or permanent residency (PR) in Canada is undoubtedly a significant milestone for me like many other immigrants. It represents an opportunity to build a life in one of the world's most sought-after destinations. However, the journey doesn't end there. For many immigrants, especially those from regulated professions like social work, healthcare, engineering, law, or finance, the path to employment is laden with challenges. One of the primary hurdles is the requirement to obtain certifications and register with professional regulatory bodies before they can practice their trade or profession.

Upon arriving in Canada, immigrants often realize that their foreign qualifications, though robust and credible in their home countries, may not meet Canadian standards. To bridge this gap, they need to undergo extensive credential evaluation processes, which often involve clearing multiple examinations, fulfilling work experience requirements, and sometimes even pursuing additional education or training programs. These processes are not only time-consuming but also financially demanding, posing a significant challenge for newcomers who are simultaneously trying to establish themselves in a new country.

Moreover, navigating the maze of certification requirements can be daunting. Each province in Canada may have its unique set of regulations for specific professions. Immigrants must familiarize themselves with these regional distinctions and adapt accordingly. The process can take months or even years, during which many highly skilled professionals are forced to take up jobs unrelated to their qualifications to sustain themselves and their families.

Another significant challenge is the lack of Canadian work experience, a factor many employers prioritize when hiring. Even immigrants with substantial expertise in their fields often find themselves at a disadvantage because they are unfamiliar with the local work culture, professional networks, and industry standards. Bridging this gap requires time, effort, and, often, mentorship or networking opportunities that are not immediately available to newcomers. The next few years were filled with the challenges of setting up a new life, learning a new culture, and adapting to a new way of living.

Living in Canada introduced me to people from all over the world. Canada is known for its diversity, with people of different backgrounds bringing their customs, foods, and traditions. It was like seeing Eastern and Western cultures mix right before me. Families like mine tried to hold on to our Indian roots while adapting to the Canadian lifestyle.

But this mix of cultures wasn't always easy. Many families felt a tug between keeping the values of their homeland and fitting into the new society. This was especially true for those with children, where parents wanted to pass on their values while helping their kids fit into Canadian life. It created a unique mix—a balance between two worlds, between the traditions of the past and the realities of the present.

 The real voyage of discovery consists not in seeking new landscapes, but having new eyes."

– Marcel Proust.

Starting fresh in Canada wasn't only about culture and practical things but getting acquainted to it.

Getting a good job, for example, often required passing exams to have our degrees recognized as mentioned above. Many of us, including myself, had to get new qualifications and slowly build our careers from scratch. It took time, patience, and a willingness to adapt to the Canadian way of life.

Yet, despite these challenges, many families found a way to make it work. We planned for our children's futures and found a sense of stability. But some of us continued to feel a connection to India, holding onto our customs and even bringing over parents or in-laws to help with childcare, making our Canadian homes feel a little like India. This balancing act—between the new and the old—was sometimes smooth, and sometimes it brought struggles, especially in raising children in a culture different from our own.

 Travel isn't always pretty. It isn't always comfortable. Sometimes, it hurts; it even breaks your heart. But that's okay. The journey changes you; it should change you."

– Anthony Bourdain.

For many immigrants like me, the journey to a new country is not just a physical relocation but also an emotional and cultural upheaval. Moving to Canada from a country like India often brings with it a sense of being caught between two worlds—a feeling of not fully belonging in either place. While Canada offers new opportunities and a promise of a better future, it also presents challenges that make integration difficult. At the same time, the emotional ties to India—the land of their roots, traditions, and memories—remain strong, creating a sense of duality that is both enriching and exhausting.

One of the primary reasons for this "in-between" feeling is the stark cultural differences. Many immigrants find solace in holding on to their traditional customs, food, and festivals as a way to preserve their identity and pass it on to their children. However, these practices often feel out of place in the Canadian context, where the culture is different and the societal norms encourage assimilation. The immigrant experience becomes a tightrope walk, balancing the desire to fit in with the need to remain connected to one's heritage.

The workplace and social life further amplify this sense of displacement. In professional settings, immigrants often encounter unfamiliar work cultures, communication styles, and expectations. These differences can lead to feelings of isolation, even as they work hard to adapt and succeed. Meanwhile, back in India, the changes in their lifestyle and perspectives can create a subtle but noticeable distance from friends and family. Visits to their homeland sometimes reveal how much they've changed, deepening the realization that they no longer fully belong there either.

For children of immigrants, the struggle is even more pronounced. They often grow up navigating two distinct worlds—the culture of their parents and the culture of their peers. This dual identity can create confusion and, at times, a sense of being torn between the two. For parents, it becomes a delicate balance of instilling traditional values while allowing their children the freedom to adapt to Canadian life.

Ultimately, the journey of immigration is as much about finding a physical home as it is about redefining one's sense of self. For those caught between two worlds, the struggle to belong is also an opportunity to grow, evolve, and craft a new identity that honors both their past and their future. Looking back, I realize that moving abroad was not only about relocating. It was about facing new challenges, learning from them, and finding a new kind of belonging. It was about the people I met, the stories they shared, and the lessons they taught me. Most of all, it was about discovering new parts of myself in a land that felt both strange and familiar. The journey is far from over, and every day brings a new chapter in this story of self-discovery.

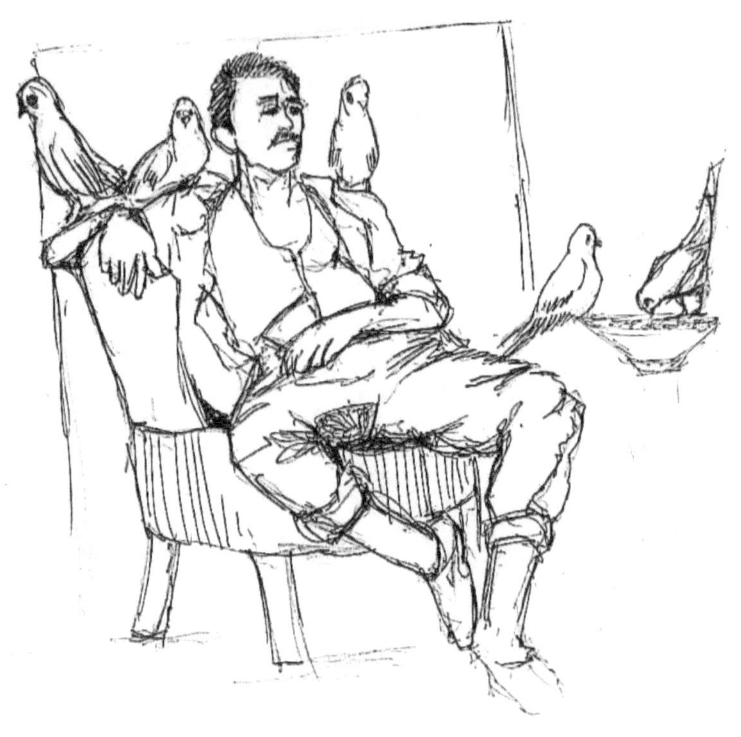

Birjee - My First Landlord

Chapter Two

Birjee - My First Landlord

When I decided to move to Canada, my visa got approved in month of August 2011, giving us nine months to make the move. The search for a home began in Toronto. We wanted a place in a good neighbourhood close to schools, stores, and shopping malls. One of my first and most pressing challenges was finding a place to stay in Canada. A friend of mine who lived in Brampton, a city near Toronto, suggested a few houses. The idea of securing a rental property seemed simple at first, but the reality was far more complex. The housing market was competitive, and affordability was just one of the many factors to consider. I had to think about proximity to good schools for my son, access to grocery stores that catered to diverse needs, reliable public transport, and a neighbourhood with a safe and welcoming environment. I tried to balance these essentials within a limited budget.

Toronto city had fewer basement apartments than cities like Mississauga, Brampton, and Milton, where most houses were large and detached, often with three to four bedrooms. These houses also had separate laundry rooms, bathrooms, and basements, making them more expensive and convenient. Many homeowners rented out their basements to make extra money. After some negotiations, we decided on a simple but practical house. My wife liked it because it was close to schools, shopping malls, and a bus stop.

Finding the right home felt like more than just ticking items off a checklist—it symbolized the first step toward stability in a foreign land. A comfortable, well-located home would mean more than shelter; it would be the foundation for our new life, a place where we could create memories and begin to belong. After looking at a few options, we found few a basement apartment with rent between CAD 800 and CAD 1500. We choose one at Mississauga. The house belonged to a Punjabi family, and the landlord's name was Birjee Singh, his real name was something else but everyone there calls him Birjee (Means big brother in Punjabi). The Punjabi community is quite large in Canada, with many neighbourhoods mostly inhabited by Punjabis. Birjee, like many Punjabis, spoke both Punjabi and Hindi fluently. His wife, however, was not as comfortable with Hindi. They had been married for five or six years then.

To come to Canada, I had to take the IELTS (International English Language Testing System) exam and get at least 6.00 bands as skilled professional, where I scored 7.0, which made getting me a visa easier. After meeting Birjee, made me curious about how others who didn't meet the English requirements managed to get visa for Canada. When I asked Birjee about it, he shared an interesting story. "This is an old story from around 2000," he said. "Back then, Girls with Canadian citizenship would marry men from other countries on a contract basis, helping them get visas and citizenship. It was quite common, and people paid agents a lot of money for such marriages."

He explained that he, too, had married a girl who had Canadian Citizenship in such a way. He paid five lakh rupees to an agent, got married, and secured a Canadian visa. But even though they were legally married, he never met the girl in person. They only exchanged documents, and within a year, the marriage ended. "You do what you have to do," he said with a shrug.

Unlike many others, Birjee wasn't well-educated. His wealth came from farming, so studying was never a priority. However, the Punjabi community in Canada supported each other a lot. He found a job as a loader in a factory. "Work is work," they say in Canada, and this principle became one of my earliest and most profound realizations after moving there in 2012. Unlike many places where certain professions are often viewed with prejudice or undervalued, Canada stood out for its genuine respect for all forms of work. Whether you were a loader moving heavy boxes, a waiter serving meals, or a janitor ensuring cleanliness, every job carried dignity, and every worker was treated with equal regard. It was a refreshing perspective, one that shifted my understanding of work and worth.

I found it fascinating that physical labor was not only respected but also often better compensated than office jobs at the time. In 2012, those involved in physical work earned between $18 and $25 an hour, while office roles typically paid around $12 to $15 an hour. This disparity reflected the value placed on hard work and the physical demands of certain jobs. It also taught me that in Canada, respect didn't stem from the title or nature of your job but from how well you performed it. People admired commitment, effort, and integrity, regardless of whether you wore a suit to work or a uniform with gloves and boots.

This ethos of respect extended beyond wages. It was evident in the way people interacted with one another—simple gestures of gratitude, polite conversations, and an absence of condescension. It reminded me that every role contributes to the functioning of society, and no work is too small or insignificant. This cultural outlook not only enriched my understanding of dignity but also inspired me to approach my own work, and those of others, with greater humility and respect. Canada taught me that the value of work is universal, and it's worth is measured not by the job title but by the honesty and effort behind it.

Two years before I moved in, Birjee had bought his own five-bedroom house. He renovated the basement and ground floor, added kitchens and bathrooms, and rented them out. After settling down, he married a girl from Punjab he had met while visiting there. However, by then, the Canadian government had tightened visa rules to prevent people from using fake marriages to immigrate. Although this marriage was genuine, his wife didn't get her visa quickly, and two years passed before she could join him.

Birjee's life became tougher throughout those two years because of his separation. He became frustrated and eventually fell into depression. To cope, he started drinking heavily and partying every weekend. His behaviour became unpredictable. When his wife finally arrived, things got better for a while, but after two years without children, the stress returned. Despite trying different treatments, they couldn't have children. Doctors said he had medical issues, which only made his drinking and partying worse.

Even after we moved in, these habits continued. Every Saturday, he insisted on having a drinking party at home, even if it wasn't right when you have rented the home and sharing with others. His brother and friends, who lived nearby, often joined in, making a lot of noise. Our move to Canada, which we thought would bring us peace, was more chaotic than we had imagined.

As time passed, it became clear that Birjee struggled to manage his work and personal life. Although he rarely talked about his problems, his mood changed noticeably. Since they had no children, adoption was not an option in their thoughts. Instead, he started breeding pigeons in the backyard. He kept about 60 to 70 pigeons, and his wife fed them water and grains every morning and night. When neighbours complained about the mess, Birjee told the authorities, "These pigeons are like my children." His explanation was accepted, and the pigeons remained a part of their lives for the next two years.

After we had been there as a tenant, Birjee and his wife wanted to go to India to meet their relatives there. He had never travelled after his wife came to Canada as both were busy making money and buying home. They both left for their village in India. He asked me to take care of the pigeons while they were away, and I did so with full responsibility. This was another experience for me to feed and water the pigeons in a given time schedule!

Despite his flaws, Birjee was a kind-hearted person who loved to serve food and drinks to his guests. He was proud of his Punjabi heritage and often spoke about the importance of the Punjabi community in Canada. *"Punjab di mitti nu nahi bhulayea ja sakda,"* he would say, meaning "You can never forget the soil of Punjab." He also shared stories about the struggles in Punjab—unemployment, drug addiction, and the challenges of those who dream of going abroad.

According to him, many Punjabis who settled in Canada faced risks when visiting Punjab again. As once they go to their village, some people would steal their visa cards and passports, blackmailing them for money. Because of this, many preferred to stay in Canada, creating a "mini Punjab" in their new country.

Punjabi migration to Canada began in the early 20th century. The first group arrived in Vancouver in 1904, mainly to work in lumber mills and on the Canadian Pacific Railway. By 1908, around 5,000 Punjabi migrants had settled in Canada, mainly in British Columbia. Over time, Punjabi communities grew in cities like Vancouver and Toronto. Today, Punjabi Canadians are one of the largest ethnic groups in the country, and their culture has become a part of Canadian society.

Punjabi Canadians have worked hard to build successful lives in Canada, contributing to the economy in various fields like business, healthcare, education, and politics. Many have become prominent figures in society. "Hard work never goes to waste," as they say, and the Punjabi community in Canada is a testament to that.

As for Birjee, he is a living example of the resilience of the Punjabi community. Despite language and culture challenges, he bought a bigger house than many others and dreamed of renting a third one. However, his struggles with the English language, especially the IELTS test, remained a sore point for him. "Kismat da khel hai," he often said, "It's all a game of fate."

In this new chapter of my life, Birjee was my first landlord—a complex man with a story that reflected the struggles and successes of the immigrant experience in Canada.

Lost Wanderer

Chapter Three

Lost Wanderer

One of the most heartening aspects of moving to Canada is discovering the numerous community organizations dedicated to helping immigrant families settle and thrive. These organizations act as pillars of support, guiding newcomers through the maze of challenges that come with starting afresh in a new country. In 2012, when I first arrived, these resources were invaluable. They provided not just practical assistance but also a sense of community that helped ease the emotional strain of leaving one's homeland behind.

Language training was often the first step in this journey. For many immigrants, fluency in English or French was not only necessary for communication but also a critical factor for securing employment and navigating daily life. Community organizations offered accessible and affordable classes tailored to different levels, ensuring that everyone, from beginners to those looking to refine their professional communication skills, had a pathway to improve. These classes also became a meeting ground, allowing newcomers to connect with others in similar situations and build friendships that alleviated feelings of isolation.

In addition to language programs, vocational training and job support services were transformative. These organizations offered workshops to help immigrants adapt their skills to the Canadian job market, write effective résumés, and prepare for interviews. They often collaborated with local businesses to provide internships or work placements, enabling immigrants to gain much-needed Canadian work experience. For families, there were resources to help enroll children in schools, access healthcare, and understand their rights and responsibilities as new residents.

While wandering in search of a job, I visited several such community organisations there. The role of these organizations in my journey cannot be overstated. I met many people there. I met Supriya Banerjee in one of such Community organisation.

Supriya and I came to Canada the same year. She was 42 years old, highly educated, and a beautiful woman. She had experience working in India in a very senior position. After our initial introduction, we exchanged phone numbers. Our struggles to find a job in Canada were similar, so we quickly became good friends.

Through our conversations, I learned more about her past. Her husband was an officer in a leading company in India, allowing them to live in a prestigious three-bedroom home in Mumbai. She had one daughter, now 20 years old. Supriya Banerjee herself had a doctorate and worked in a well-known corporate. Her family life seemed settled. Her husband had few close relatives, as he was an only child. His parents had passed away in his childhood, and he had studied and secured a job by staying in a hostel in Mumbai. Supriya's father, now 70, lived alone in Kolkata. He was a retired Employee from a reputed institution.

However, her life took a drastic turn when her husband died suddenly of a heart attack. Supriya's daughter was eight years old;. He didn't even have time to reach the hospital. For the first few months after her husband died, many of her husband's friends came to help her. Initially they were helped her a lot. But slowly it became impossible. But gradually their help and meeting also decreased, but as months passed this support gradually disappeared. Despite being a husband, Supriya Banerjee did not have the support of any of her in-laws. And she didn't even know anyone. And also when the husband died, no one came to look after her. Supriya, too, gradually adjusted. She began to get involved in her job and daughter's lives.

Supriya continued to work at the job, but the sympathy from her colleagues made her feel uncomfortable. What once was respect turned into pity, making her acutely aware of her vulnerability. She began to feel the need for a fresh start and considered remarrying, not just for herself but also to ensure her daughter's safety and well-being.

Yet, in India, she felt that finding a suitable partner would be difficult, especially without the full support of her community. She knew she needed a change. With her qualifications and experience, she believed she could find opportunities abroad. So, she applied for a visa to Canada and was accepted along with her daughter. Both Supriya and her daughter arrived in Canada as soon as the visa application procedure was over, her daughter then just entered in College then and was living in hostel. Supriya asked her daughter to continue in India with her studies till she gets proper employment in Canada. College or University education being expensive in Canada she thought leaving her daughter to continue her education in India.

Alone in a new country, Supriya faced the harsh reality of the job market. She had been in a respected profession in India, but her qualifications didn't hold the same value in Canada. Permanent residency was one thing, but finding a job in her field was another challenge. She had to take certified courses to meet Canadian standards and started working as an office assistant to cover her expenses. She quickly realized that establishing herself in this new society would take more time and effort.

After a few months, an Indian businessman in Canada recognized her potential and offered her a job as his secretary. He paid her just $12 an hour and occasionally sponsored her breakfast and lunch. The businessman, a 55-year-old divorcee, saw Supriya as a potential partner. He tried to woo her with gifts and fancy dinners, but Supriya was disgusted by his advances. She was not interested in marrying someone much older, especially someone who seemed more attracted to her looks than to her as a person.

During this time, Supriya also worked with another Indian man who asked her to design professional courses for his private college. She worked hard, creating course modules that were eventually approved by the government, allowing her to start teaching. However, she wasn't paid for designing the courses, and her teaching job didn't pay much either. Like many other immigrants, Supriya found her skills and experience were undervalued, and she struggled to make ends meet.

Despite these challenges, Supriya never compromised on her values. She continued taking courses and eventually landed a more stable job. However, the search for companionship was still on her mind. She tried online friendship and matrimonial sites and eventually met a tall, handsome American soldier stationed overseas. They communicated regularly through video calls, and after two months, he expressed a desire to visit her in Toronto. He seemed like the perfect match, and Supriya was excited at the prospect of finally finding someone to share her life with.

She spent weeks planning for his arrival, dreaming of their future together. But he didn't show up on the day he was supposed to arrive. Instead, he called her with a story about a terrorist attack at his base, claiming that all his belongings had been stolen and he needed money to book a new ticket. Supriya immediately grew suspicious. She had heard about online scams and realized that she might be dealing with a fraudster. She consulted with friends, who confirmed her suspicions. When she told the man she didn't have money to send him but she can surely help once he come to Toronto. She will take care of all his expenses there, after this response, he disappeared, cutting off all contacts and Facebook accounts. Even after that, several people approached her online with grand promises, but none were genuine, leaving her with a profound sense of disappointment and loneliness. This ordeal left her wondering if true love or genuine connection would ever be hers.

Supriya decided to invest in real estate, lured by the promise of significant profits. Many courses were available on the subject, and she enrolled in one hoping to grow her savings. But gradually, she realized that those running these courses weren't investors themselves but simply profiting from teaching others. The information provided was often unreliable, and Supriya lost more than she earned. To invest in this venture, she had taken out loans and even withdrawn funds through an overdraft. Eventually, she exhausted her savings, her loans piled up, and her trainer disappeared after defrauding hundreds of people.

Meanwhile, her daughter, now a young adult, had completed her post-graduation. Supriya invited her to live together, hoping they could share a home in Canada. But her daughter, who had grown independent and used to hostel life over the past five years, chose to live separately even in the same city. Supriya felt deeply saddened. Now grown up and hardly needing her mother's companionship, her daughter showed little interest in reconnecting closely. When she came to Canada, her daughter chose to rent a separate place. Her young, intelligent daughter quickly found a suitable job and even adopted two cats. Supriya had come to Canada with dreams of a fresh, beautiful life, but nothing happened as she had imagined amidst all these experiences and challenges. Although Supriya had envisioned their reunion differently, her daughter visited only occasionally, more like a guest than family. The growing distance was painful for Supriya, who longed for the close connection they once shared.

In her quest for stability, Supriya found herself drawn to a Christian religious group. She joined them, hoping that a new faith might bring her inner peace and guidance in her journey. Every Wednesday and Sunday, she attended church prayers and publicly expressed her devotion on social media. This spiritual path, however, didn't lead to the contentment she had expected. The restlessness had not settled. Throughout this journey, she neither found a life partner nor the closeness she once had with her daughter. She also couldn't find the golden career and respect she had in India, and now, age was catching up with her.

After many years of effort, Supriya finally secured a stable job. Her daughter continued living independently, visiting occasionally. Despite all the changes, Supriya still hadn't found a life partner. Now, her daughter was nearing marriageable age, and Supriya realized that what she had come to Canada searching for was slipping away from her grasp.

Supriya's pursuit seemed forever out of reach, teasing her at every turn. She now found herself drifting into a different world, where even on social media, there was no one proposing, and marriage seemed an elusive prospect. As it happens, when certain needs go unmet, one eventually lets go, telling oneself, "Let it be," and finds solace in other things. In her case, however, the journey felt like complete failure and disappointment.

In one's own country, like India, people enjoy a support system—a familiar neighbourhood, a shared language, and people who understand each other. Canada had held promises of opportunity and growth, but what had Supriya truly found in all of this? Reflecting on it, I couldn't help but feel a deep sadness for her. Her dream of building a fulfilling life seemed to have misfired, and now, Supriya was merely going through the motions of life, as if living at the bottom of an empty well.

"Wherever you go in the world, women face similar struggles," I thought. There's an underlying cause for the suffering of women everywhere—simply that they are women. Those women who manage to break free do so against the odds, yet society is rarely willing to let them live in peace, pulling them back in countless ways.

This was Supriya's story in Canada—a journey that started with hope, but met resistance every step of the way.

Reflecting on her journey, Supriya couldn't help but feel that her life had become like an empty well, devoid of fulfilment and connection. The struggle had aged her, leaving her with the unsettling realization that, despite her efforts, life hadn't unfolded as she hoped. "A woman's fate is to navigate these unending trials," she mused, considering how, no matter where they go in the world, many women face the same battles in different forms.

Always Present to Help!

Chapter Four

Always Present to Help!

In Canada, finding a job as a newcomer can feel like a full-time commitment, often requiring as much energy and effort as the job itself. The process begins with scouring job boards, online portals, and community bulletin boards, each promising opportunities but often requiring skills or experience that seem just out of reach. For many, it also means walking into offices or stores, résumés in hand, hoping for a chance to make a personal connection. Every application, every form filled, every interview feels like a small victory, but the road to employment is rarely straightforward. In those early days, persistence becomes a way of life, as does learning to handle rejection gracefully while maintaining optimism.

The hustle is compounded by the reality that, in Canada, no one is waiting to help you land your dream job. Everyone is busy with their own lives, and while there are community support workers and career counsellors stationed in accessible locations, their role is primarily to guide rather than hand over opportunities. They can help you refine your résumé, suggest job leads, or coach you for interviews, but there are no guarantees. The onus of success lies squarely on the individual's shoulders. Those who secure their first job often describe the moment as euphoric, akin to touching the sky. The sense of achievement is immense, particularly after enduring the relentless grind of applications and interviews.

What's remarkable is how these early job experiences ripple through immigrant communities. The lessons learned—whether it's navigating the online job portals, tailoring applications to Canadian expectations, or succeeding in interviews—become stories and strategies shared generously with newcomers. It's almost a tradition: those who succeed make it their mission to guide others, passing on tips, leads, and encouragement. Yet, for many, the first job is just a stepping stone. Even as they work diligently in their initial roles, they aspire for better opportunities, dreaming of jobs that align more closely with their qualifications and passions.

In the midst of this journey, I heard about a Marathi man (A person from Maharashtra) living in Mississauga. This man is known for helping others without seeking anything in return and has many local connections. I finally got his phone number and grew curious about meeting this man, who had an almost mythical reputation. After two long bus rides, I found myself in his office.

He greeted me with a welcoming smile—a middle-aged, stout man with a cheerful face. He was around six feet tall, with a stocky build, a shirt that struggled to contain his belly pressing against his belt, and a tie barely held in place. His hair was balding at the back and neatly combed up front, and there was a striking expression in his eyes. He greeted me with a warm handshake and ordered tea from an office machine, one of the best cups I'd had here. This was Shrikant Prabhu—a warm, sincere, open-hearted man who was known to help anyone in need, especially first-time immigrants. Without hesitation, he would even take out money from his own pocket to buy someone a meal.

In Canada, especially in the nearby cities to Toronto, there isn't an efficient public transportation system like Mumbai or like other cities back home. Some places are only accessible by car. When I had an interview or needed to get somewhere, Shrikant Prabhu himself would drive me there in his car. Right from our first meeting, I was impressed by his warm, generous nature. He was doing well in his business, seemed to be financially comfortable, and loved fine food. Always carrying the key to an exclusive and very pricey gym in his hand, he made sure it was seen by everyone he met. I began meeting him more often, as I had a lot of free time, and he seemed to enjoy my company too.

Shrikant did have one quirk: he enjoyed talking about himself with grand exaggeration, constantly hinting at how important he was. Personal information didn't stay personal with him, and he would openly share details about those he knew. People often joked, "If Shrikant knows something, and the whole city of Canada will know it too."

Shrikant Prabhu believes he exists to "teach people a lesson" and seems to take Gandhi's phrase, "Lead them to wisdom and leave them," as his personal motto. Whatever the topic, Shrikant has a firm opinion, and he insists others must accept it, whether they agree or not. Over time, people tend to become cautious around him, trying to avoid his insistence on being heard. His constant "lessons" can feel irritating or even insulting to some, but he continues to help people regardless. Many connections came and went with Shrikant, and over time, our friendship grew closer. Shrikant confided in me about his life, eventually sharing his background and his journey from Mumbai to Canada.

Shrikant was originally from Mumbai, where he completed his B.Com and then accepted a job as a hotel manager in Gujarat after graduation. He came to Canada after his marriage. Shrikant's wife, Vini, had met him during their college years. While studying B.Com at a prestigious

Mumbai college, Shrikant was an active leader in the student union, loved participating in cultural events, and even enjoyed singing. In his second year, a new girl named Vini joined the advertising department. She was from North India and had moved to Mumbai for her studies. Her beauty and distinctive northern charm quickly made her a topic of interest in college. Some friends even placed bets on who would win her over, and Shrikant took up the challenge.

Shrikant went to impressive lengths to befriend Vini, emulating the bold efforts often seen in Bollywood movies of that era. Eventually, Vini and he became close, and soon their love was well-known across campus. They graduated, yet their love story continued. Shrikant moved to Gujarat for work, but he and Vini stayed in touch, meeting whenever they could.

Srikanth and Vini finally decided to get married. Vini's family, being North Indian, strongly opposed their marriage. But Shrikant was determined. He stood his ground and married her despite opposition from his family. Shrikant came from a traditional Konkani household, while Vini had a culturally different background. As it often happens, these differences surfaced after marriage, and the marriage proved more challenging than he'd expected. Vini, raised in a family that practiced emotional blackmail to assert authority, often clashed with Shrikant's mother, who commanded her own level of respect. His mother, a single parent who had lost her husband young, had raised Shrikant and his two brothers with sheer strength and determination.

After marriage, frequent arguments flared between his mother and Vini. Shrikant, stuck between his wife and mother, struggled to maintain peace. He sought family intervention and tried other means to restore harmony, but nothing seemed to work. Hoping that having children might bring stability, he and Vini had two daughters. However, the situation at home grew increasingly volatile. His mother was aging, and her constant stress weighed heavily on Shrikant. He found himself staying longer hours in Gujarat for work, but he knew this was no permanent solution.

Shrikant thought a change of environment might improve things. "Maybe if we move to a new place, she'll change," he told himself. However, leaving his mother alone was impossible, and he didn't want to face the judgment of relatives and neighbours'. Finally, he considered a more radical solution: a move abroad. Shrikant reasoned that if he and Vini could be together away from family and familiar ties, perhaps they could settle down peacefully.

Shrikant was highly successful in his hotel career, so he felt confident that he could manage work abroad. His children were still young and could adapt, he believed. With a firm plan in mind, he convinced Vini to consider a move to Canada, presenting the idea as a new beginning for them both. Vini, a trained medical professional, also saw the potential for work abroad. And with this, the two of them packed up their lives and moved to Canada, setting out to rebuild and find peace in a new world.

Arriving in Canada, Shrikant Prabhu quickly realized that his journey would be more challenging than expected. Despite his hotel management experience, he didn't land a job immediately. "Canada can be slow to open doors," he thought as he settled into a temporary sales position, doing just enough to cover expenses. Thankfully, he'd saved a substantial amount before arriving, allowing him to weather the early days without too much strain. Meanwhile, Vini needed to complete additional certifications to work in the healthcare sector, so she was at home searching for the right courses. Their daughters, though, settled into school smoothly, thanks to Canada's mandatory education system.

In those initial months, Canada was hit by a healthcare crisis that left hospitals short-staffed. In response, the government relaxed its regulations, allowing healthcare workers with relevant experience to begin work immediately, with credential verification to follow. This unexpected development turned into an opportunity for Vini, who soon secured a job in a local hospital. "Finally, things are falling into place," Shrikant thought as they began to settle into a routine. However, he found adapting to Canadian workplace culture both demanding and draining. Balancing this with the adjustments at home was no easy feat.

With Vini earning a substantial income, her behaviour soon reverted to its earlier patterns, and their relationship grew strained. Her confidence in her financial independence made her believe she no longer needed Shrikant's support. "Who needs a partner when you're financially self-sufficient?" she seemed to imply. Gradually, she even began to suggest that Shrikant could stay home rather than work, hinting that his presence was more of a hindrance than a support. It seemed she had grown comfortable dictating the terms of their relationship.

Vini's job as hospital staff paid well, which only strengthened her sense of independence. With a stable income, she started to view Shrikant's career efforts as unnecessary. She wanted full control over her earnings and expected Shrikant to follow suit. Emotionally, their connection began to erode, and their marriage seemed to be heading toward an inevitable end. "The very reason I came to Canada—to rebuild our life together—has crumbled," Shrikant reflected bitterly.

Fortunately, the distance spared his mother from the brunt of their issues, though he himself felt emotionally cornered. Despite the instability, Shrikant was meticulously organized. "I came here with a purpose, and I'm determined to stand on my own feet, no matter what," he resolved. Shrikant remained financially independent, refusing to rely on Vini's earnings. He maintained a dignified distance, his pride unyielding.

Financial independence gave Vini an inflated sense of autonomy. She dismissed any need for external control or partnership, seeing herself as her own authority. Unlike Shrikant, who had experienced painful setbacks, Vini's traditional mindset kept her rooted in certain boundaries, and she never engaged in extramarital relationships. However, Shrikant, perhaps seeking solace, eventually pursued other connections, finding a temporary sense of belonging through relationships with women he encountered. While these relationships offered a semblance of comfort, they could never replace the respect and companionship he once yearned for.

Ultimately, Shrikant realized that his deepest grievance wasn't physical intimacy or financial independence but a lack of respect from his partner.

Shrikant Prabhu's journey to Canada, initially fuelled by dreams of building a successful life and family, became a lesson in resilience, adaptation, and the shifting sands of relationships. Determined to carve out a new beginning in the hospitality industry, he found himself navigating unforeseen challenges. Despite trying his best to create a stable and happy home life, Shrikant's ideal family vision remained unfulfilled. His struggle in the professional realm mirrored the turbulence at home.

Initially unable to establish himself in his chosen field, Shrikant turned to other ventures to support his family. "Adapt or fall behind," he thought, taking on various roles—some which succeeded, others which failed. Eventually, through connections and guidance, he ventured into the world of investments. After acquiring the necessary certifications, Shrikant made his mark as an investment consultant and soon found a foothold. His network grew, and so did his confidence. "Canada teaches you to survive in ways you never imagined," he often remarked.

Meanwhile, as their daughters grew up and found their paths, the strain between Shrikant and Vini increased. They chose to pursue a divorce, despite counselling advice to work through their issues. "Maybe the tension had built up for too long," Shrikant reflected, acknowledging that neither of them had ever genuinely addressed their differences. Instead, they focused on solving each other's problems without resolving their own. Their unresolved conflicts left a lingering impact on their children, who watched their parents' struggles and learned their own lessons in resilience.

Post-divorce, Shrikant found himself facing new challenges as a single parent, with his children alternating time between him and their mother. "They know how to get what they want from us," he observed, realizing that his children had adapted to the split in their own ways. Despite the distance in the family, Shrikant continued to focus on his career. His investment business thrived, and he used his success to give back to the community, something he had always valued deeply.

Yet, amid the outward success, Shrikant dealt with his own emotional voids. Food became his comfort, and every breakfast was shared with a guest—a new friend, a colleague, or a mentor. These shared meals were, in a way, his antidote to loneliness, as he filled his mornings with conversation and connection. "Sometimes, we fill the emptiness with what's in front of us," he thought, acknowledging the comfort these meals brought.

In recent years, though, he had taken strides to address his health, realizing that he needed to take control not just of his career but also of his well-being. Shrikant even considered returning to India, exploring the possibility during a visit. "Could I really adjust back home after all these years?" he pondered, questioning if the culture he had left behind would now feel foreign. And then there was the nagging doubt: would returning to India feel like defeat?

Shrikant's family dreams had been grand—a close-knit, united family—but his reality looked different. While he had a successful career and strong community ties, his family remained divided. "What does it mean to truly succeed in family life?" he often wondered. Today, he finds himself contemplating what happiness really entails, recognizing that some dreams may remain "beautifully empty."

In the end, Shrikant's Canadian journey was more than an external adventure; it was a deep exploration of his values, strengths, and the intricate dynamics of human relationships. Through it all, he continued to build, adapt, and grow, even as the shape of his dreams changed.

A Summer in Canada

Chapter Five

A Summer in Canada

Summer in Canada is not just a season; it's a celebration—a time when life bursts forth with vibrant energy and people come together to embrace the beauty of nature. For a country known for its long, cold winters that often stretch over seven to eight months, summer offers a much-needed reprieve. It's a time to shed layers of clothing and the constraints of indoor living, stepping out to feel the sun on your skin and breathe in the fresh, open air. While winter sports like skiing and snowboarding are popular, they remain inaccessible luxuries for many, either due to cost or location. For the majority, summer becomes the true equalizer, offering everyone, regardless of circumstance, a chance to revel in the outdoors.

Canadian summers bring people to the heart of nature—parks, lakes, and trails—places that feel alive with activity and camaraderie. Parks, in particular, hold a special charm. These spaces are thoughtfully designed, offering more than just greenery. They are equipped with barbeque areas for family gatherings, clean restrooms that make spending an entire day outdoors convenient, and well-maintained cycling tracks that wind through scenic landscapes. In summer, parks transform into vibrant hubs where laughter echoes, children play freely, and friends bond over shared meals. For solo explorers, they offer a tranquil escape, a chance to reflect amidst the rustling leaves and chirping birds.

What makes Canadian summers truly magical is how they bring people together. Whether its strangers chatting while waiting for a grill to heat up, cyclists exchanging tips on the best trails, or families sharing picnic spots with newfound friends, nature becomes a unifying force. It reminds people of the simple joys—watching a sunset, feeling the cool grass underfoot, or hearing the splash of water at a lake's edge. In a world often consumed by screens and deadlines, summer in Canada feels like a gentle nudge to pause, connect, and celebrate the present moment.

For newcomers like me in 2012, experiencing a Canadian summer was like stepping into a new rhythm of life. It wasn't just about enjoying the warm weather; it was about discovering a culture that treasures its seasons, makes the most of its fleeting warmth, and finds unity in the beauty of nature. Summer is a gift, and in Canada, it's celebrated with a spirit that's contagious and unforgettable. One day in a summer, I and my wife and my son decided to visit one of these parks. As we walked along the park's shaded trails, my son suddenly called out to his mother—Aai - in Marathi, our native language. His voice echoed in the park, catching the attention of another family nearby. They heard the familiar words and immediately turned to find us.

"In unfamiliar places, a familiar word or face can feel like home."

In a foreign land, there's something magical about hearing your own language. It creates an instant connection, a sense of familiarity that warms your heart. The family approached us with wide smiles, introducing themselves as fellow Maharashtrians. It was an instant bond, as though we had known them for years.

The head of the family, Mr. Dongre, was a man in his sixties with a lean frame, graying hair, and a gentle demeanor. He wore glasses that framed his sharp, expressive eyes. Dressed neatly and exuding a warm and friendly vibe, he was accompanied by his wife and their son, Sumit who appeared to be in his early twenties. They greeted us and we spent good time in park. They exchanged their contact details and address and mentioned that they will be happy to support us in case we need any support.

During our discussion with the family at the park, I notice something unusual about Sumit, the young son of Mr. and Mrs. Dongre. His movements and manner of speaking hinted at something different, something that set him apart. There was a condition, but I couldn't immediately figure out what it was.

As our conversation progressed, we got to know more about the Dongres. Originally from Mumbai, they had moved to Canada about ten years ago. Mr. Dongre was a skilled engineer who had held a prestigious position in Mumbai before moving. Their elder daughter was bright and academically inclined. Then came the story of Sumit, their second child.

Summit's birth, they said, was perfectly normal. He grew up like any other child—his development was on track, and he was doing well in school. But one day, out of nowhere, everything changed. He had his first seizure. That moment turned their world upside down.

Doctors diagnosed him with epilepsy and revealed something that no parent would want to hear: Sumit had been born with an underlying weakness that had gone unnoticed until the seizures began. The news shattered their confidence, but they did everything they could to support him.

"The strength of a family is often measured by how they come together during difficult times."

Doctors had explained that in many cases, epilepsy can be controlled with proper treatment, and individuals with this condition can go on to live normal lives. But at the time, they had failed to convey this hope clearly to the Dongres. Instead, the family was left with the fear that Sumit would always be fragile and in need of constant care.

Over time, the Dongres' entire life began to revolve around Sumit. He became the focal point of their family. Every decision they made, every conversation, and every action seemed to be centered on him. Their focus was so intense that, instead of enabling Sumit to grow stronger, they unknowingly made him dependent on them. Their worry turned into overprotection, and their intention of shielding him from harm inadvertently limited his ability to develop independence. Mr. Dongre admitted that they might have overly sheltered Sushmit, not realizing that their intense worry and care had kept him dependent.

"Sometimes, life pushes us to move, not just places, but perspectives too."

Sushmit, the younger son of the Dongres, had slowly realized that he was the center of attention in his household. Over time, this awareness turned into dominance. Whenever he was asked to study or help with any household chores, he would throw tantrums, shout at his family, and become aggressive. His behavior began to intimidate everyone at home.

As Sushmit grew older, his health and temper became more unpredictable. His epilepsy worsened, and his emotional outbursts started to affect the family's daily life. Relatives and neighbors frequently asked about his condition, often offering sympathy or unsolicited advice. The constant questions and judgment made life even more stressful for the Dongres.

"Sometimes, change isn't just a choice—it becomes a necessity."

Around this time, the family decided to move. Mrs. Dongre's sister, who lived in Canada, suggested they consider relocating there. Canada, she said, was known for its excellent healthcare system and inclusive environment. It might offer Sushmit better treatment and a chance to become more independent. After much deliberation, the Dongres decided to take a leap of faith and move to Canada.

Moving to Canada wasn't easy, but the Dongres were resourceful and determined. Shortly after arriving, they connected with a local Marathi group, which turned out to be a blessing. This group was a vibrant community of people from their home state, celebrating festivals like Ganpati, Dussehra, Diwali, and Holi with enthusiasm. For the Dongres, this was a wonderful way to stay connected to their roots while adapting to life in a new country.

"A strong community can make any place feel like home."

Through this group, the Dongres not only celebrated festivals but also made lasting friendships. Their involvement in these events provided a sense of belonging and helped them embrace their new life in Canada.

Interestingly, my time in Canada also brought a change in me. Back in Mumbai, I rarely participated in festivals or cultural events. The noise and crowds never appealed to me. But during my four years in Canada, I found myself attending every celebration, eager to meet people and share stories. It was during one such gathering that I reconnected with the Dongres again.

Our first meeting had been brief—an exchange of pleasantries at the park. But this time, our interaction deepened. Over the months, we met regularly and became good friends. Their warmth, hospitality, and shared love for Marathi culture made me feel at home in a foreign land.

Finding a suitable and affordable home in Canada can be a daunting task. My first rented house had served me well for two years, but as time passed, the landlord's unreasonable demands and constant interference became unbearable. It was time to move. We reached out to a family we knew, asking for suggestions about a new place to stay. To our relief, they not only offered advice but also helped us secure a new home. Packing our belongings, we made the move and settled into a more peaceful environment. It was during this time that I began crossing paths with the Dongres more frequently.

As we met on various occasions, I grew closer to their son, Sumit. Over time, Mr. Dongre shared with me the struggles and challenges they had faced as a family.

Sushmit's health had been fragile since childhood, and his parents had made the bold decision to immigrate to

Canada with the hope of finding better medical treatment for him. Upon arriving in Canada, they explored numerous treatments and therapies. However, none brought the results they had hoped for. Time passed, and as Sumit grew older, his willpower and desire to recover began to diminish.

He became accustomed to a sedentary lifestyle, gaining weight and losing the strength to perform even simple tasks. Walking short distances, lifting light weights, or doing small household chores began to feel burdensome for him. A condition that might have been manageable in its earlier stages had now become a significant obstacle.

"When life becomes comfortable, sometimes the fight to improve fades away."

Over time, Sushmit grew reliant on the disability benefits provided by the Canadian government. These monthly payments were generous enough for an individual to live modestly. While the family did not need this financial support—Mr. Dongre was a successful engineer earning a good salary—the assistance gave Sumit a sense of independence.

The Dongres had built a stable and comfortable life in Canada. They owned their home, had a car, and enjoyed the conveniences of modern living. However, Sumit's condition remained a source of concern. His dependence on government support and his unwillingness to push himself toward recovery were realities the family had come to accept.

After Sushmit began receiving a disability allowance in Canada, all efforts to improve his health and condition came to a halt. Sumit was quick to understand one thing: whether he needed help or not, his family was always ready to care for him. Over time, he learned that by acting helpless, he could avoid any responsibilities or tasks. If he showed even the slightest sign of effort, his parents would shield him from anything challenging.

"The line between care and enabling dependency is often blurred by love."

Friends and well-wishers repeatedly advised Mr. and Mrs. Dongre that their excessive protection was doing more harm than good. "You're spoiling Sumit," they would say. But the Dongres would respond with, "Babu is delicate, you know," and continue to coddle him.

Over the years, Sushmit had become entirely reliant on his family, with no motivation to improve his life. Mr. Dongre began to realize, albeit very late, that his son was taking them for granted and had no intention of taking charge of his own life. The realization hit him hard: "Sumit is now beyond the point of change, and we've grown too old to manage him forever."

In Canada, retirement age is 65, and Mr. Dongre was only two years away from it. He regretted not addressing Sushmit's dependency earlier when there might still have been hope. By now, Sushmit had settled into a life of comfort: spending most of his time on the sofa, watching TV, eating, and following cricket.

Sushmit was exceptionally intelligent and had an encyclopaedic knowledge of cricket. He could discuss cricket history, players from different countries, their statistics, and records in remarkable detail. However, despite his knowledge, he had never played cricket himself—not even as a child. *"Every person has a unique talent, but talent without action is wasted potential."*

Friends and peers of the Dongres tried to engage with Sushmit. Some of his contemporaries even attempted to motivate him, but nothing worked. Meanwhile, his elder sister graduated, found a job, and eventually got married.

Sushmit, however, remained stagnant. He grew older, but he didn't grow up. The idea of taking charge of his own life, or working toward independence, never crossed his mind. The disability allowance provided him with a safety net, and the motivation to strive for a better life slowly faded. Sumit's parents hoped that he would one day stand on his own feet, but deep down, they began to accept that he never would. Even when Sushmit expressed interest in trying something new or looking for a job, his own parents discouraged him, saying, "Are you sure you can handle it? What if it's too hard for you?" They didn't realize that their lack of confidence in him was pushing him further into inaction.

When Sushmit attempted to work at a local store, his parents became overly protective. "What if something happens to you?" they would say, and eventually, he gave up the idea entirely. Their fears and hesitations robbed Sushmit of opportunities to grow, and their overprotectiveness became his greatest limitation.

Mr. Dongre's daughter, now married, lives nearby in the same Canadian city. Whenever she has plans to go out, she leaves her young children with her parents. Looking after little ones is no easy task, but the Dongres willingly take up the responsibility. However, there is a traditional undertone to this dynamic. Despite living in a progressive and individualistic society like Canada, the Indian cultural expectations of grandparents helping with childcare still persist. Their daughter, though modern and educated, rarely asks her parents if they are comfortable with this arrangement. For her, it's almost expected that her parents will help, as this is how things have always worked in their Indian upbringing.

Now, Mr. Dongre is 74, and his wife is 69. They are still healthy and active, which is a blessing. Financially, they are secure with their own house, a stable retirement income, and savings. Yet, as they age, they begin to feel the weight of responsibility that has lingered far longer than they anticipated. Mr. Dongre often reflects on how life turned out. He and his wife regularly attend community events, seek joy in small moments, and immerse themselves in social activities to distract from their inner worries. In quiet moments, though, he admits to close friends the mistakes they made in raising their son, Sushmit. They had hoped that moving to Canada would bring them happiness and prosperity, but now they wonder if staying in India might have been better.

"Sometimes, the life you escape from is the one that holds the answers you seek."

Back in India, the social structure and societal pressure might have pushed Sushmit to take responsibility for his life. In Canada, however, the comfort of a disability allowance and the absence of social expectations allowed him to settle into a life of dependency. Mr. Dongre now realizes that Sushmit cannot easily adapt to either world. He is neither capable of thriving in India's demanding social fabric nor financially equipped to handle Canada's rising cost of living on his own. This leaves the Dongres with an unending worry: "What will happen to Sushmit after us?"

The luxurious lifestyle that Canada offers has come with its own challenges. The Dongres are left wondering if they unknowingly sacrificed their peace for this prosperity. With Sushmit unprepared to handle life's demands, the family's story raises an important question about how cultural expectations, financial systems, and parental decisions shape the future of children.

For Mr. Dongre, the journey to Canada has been one of mixed blessings. While it brought comfort and stability, it also left him questioning the choices that shaped their family's future. Now, in his twilight years, he finds solace in moments of gratitude but remains tethered to the anxieties of what lies ahead.

"Sometimes life brings unexpected storms, and the courage to navigate them defines who we are."

Successful Businessman

Chapter Six

Successful Businessman

In Canada, I found myself among countless newcomers, all striving for stability and a path forward in a land of promise. Large community centers dedicated to supporting immigrants were a beacon of hope. These centers offered an array of free services—career counselling, language courses, and skill development programs—all tailored to help newcomers navigate the complexities of their new lives. Inside, you could find computers to update résumés, shelves filled with books to borrow, photocopiers for essential documents, and even free stationery. These bustling hubs were filled with a palpable sense of determination, as hopeful faces sought guidance and opportunities. In my early days, I, too, walked into one of these centers, eager to equip myself with the tools needed to find my footing in this unfamiliar world.

The YMCA, in particular, became a cornerstone of my initial journey. Their courses, thoughtfully designed for immigrants, focused on integration into Canadian society, offering training in job searches, business skills, and more. I enrolled in one such program held in a vibrant building that housed a multitude of activities and even a private community college. During breaks, we often gathered at the Tim Hortons café conveniently located on the ground floor—a quintessential Canadian experience.

One afternoon, as I sipped my coffee amidst the buzz of conversation, a familiar sound caught my attention. A woman at a nearby table was speaking on the phone in

Marathi, my mother tongue. The moment felt surreal—a small yet profound reminder of home in the midst of a bustling Canadian city. Her voice carried fragments of a conversation about the challenges of securing a job and the various courses designed to ease the process for newcomers. It was a striking moment, bridging the gap between two worlds: the struggles of starting afresh in Canada and the comforting familiarity of my roots.

That day, in the heart of a foreign land, I realized how shared experiences and connections—no matter how fleeting—could make even the most daunting transitions feel a little less lonely. Moments like these became a quiet reassurance that I wasn't alone in this journey and that the path forward, though challenging, was one many had walked before me.

Intrigued, I approached her after the call. She was a professional-looking woman in her late 40s, with a sharp appearance that included a corporate-style sari paired with a black coat. Introducing herself as Madhavi Deshmukh, she was the first Marathi professional I'd met in Canada. She worked as a marketing manager at a private placement agency and was deeply knowledgeable about the Canadian job market.

"Getting a job here isn't easy," she said, smiling knowingly. "You'll need to take some local courses—Canadian qualifications matter far more than anything from abroad." I explained that I was still job-hunting after four months in the country, and she nodded sympathetically. She then offered, "If you take a course and then pay my agency's placement fee, I can help you secure a job."

Taking her advice to heart, I decided to visit a private career college. I met with a counsellor who outlined various options, such as project management, business analysis, and Six Sigma. The fees were high, but Canadian government support made it possible: They would cover the tuition, and I would receive a monthly living allowance of 800 Canadian dollars as part of the training.

Reflecting on it, I thought, "What's the harm in learning something new, especially if I'm getting some financial assistance?" Convinced, I enrolled in a business management course, which would not only cover my expenses but also improve my employability. The college, receiving $11,000 per student, was incentivized to help people get jobs, and the monthly allowance was a lifeline.

It wasn't until the end of the course that I realized the true cost of this financial aid: the education loan would have to be repaid, with the exception of the living allowance. "In the end, there are no free lunches," I thought to myself as I began repaying the loan. In my first year in Canada, I'd gained experience, new skills, and a clearer picture of how things worked. Though I was a little older and perhaps a little wiser, I knew that this journey was just beginning.

Madhavi a marketing manager, a person with sharp eye for talent. Her role was essentially to bring in clients for her company, often immigrants desperate for stable employment. She had a sharp talent for persuasion, offering hopeful promises to those eager to start a new life, in exchange for service fees that ranged from $500 to $1,000.

Madhavi was a remarkable professional, bringing clients in with ease and conviction. I later realized that these private placement companies often targeted newly arrived immigrants like myself, creating a business out of the aspirations of countless individuals. "The game was about making money," I reflected, "not really about helping anyone build a career." While these agencies had polished programs and courses on paper, the actual teaching was subpar, often led by those themselves struggling to establish a foothold in Canada.

Soon, I found a part-time job that eased my expenses and allowed me to gain some independence. My resentment towards the college eventually dissipated, as my interactions with Madhavi continued. We often discussed work and life in Canada, and, in time, Madhavi became a close friend, a constant presence through the trials of settling in.

Madhavi, as I learned, had a resilient and tenacious spirit. She was born and raised in Maharashtra, India, the eldest of three siblings. Excelling in academics, she completed her engineering degree with top honours. She married a successful Marathi man, but their life was far from ideal as her marriage brought its own struggles after facing familial pressure and personal challenges, they decided to relocate to Canada for a fresh start.

Canada was a new beginning for her. Initially, she worked as a part-time lecturer in a local college but soon realized it wasn't financially sustainable. Her true skill was marketing, and soon, she took on a full-time role as a marketing manager in a placement company.

While in India, she had experience and enjoyed doing plays, lectures and other stage shows, so she discovered and hosted community radio in Canada, as well as lecturing elsewhere. Even in Canada, she started giving lectures in different slums and community centres. She used to convince people how they can get a good job easily, if they join her company. Her language skills—fluent in Marathi, Hindi, Gujarati, English, and even some Punjabi—enabled her to connect with various communities, especially immigrants and homemakers seeking educational opportunities. Her approach was straightforward; she would highlight how learning through government-supported programs would bring financial assistance and potentially lead to employment.

"Learning is the ticket to freedom here," she often said, tapping into people's aspirations. In many cases, people weren't entirely misled—there was genuine financial aid and potential to gain skills. But the hidden costs, like the loans one would eventually need to repay, weren't as transparent. Many found themselves tangled in debt over time, paying back what they thought was financial aid.

Interestingly, some families encouraged their wives to enrol in these programs. For some, education opened doors to better job opportunities, while for others, it simply meant using the funds as leverage to purchase a home, a car, or other essentials, even if the courses themselves held little value.

Many people I met were trying their best to navigate the system, seeking stability in either jobs or businesses, yet, there was a lingering undercurrent of caution. The talk of "consultancy fees" and "courses" came up frequently. Some newcomers, unaware, were caught up in cycles of paying hefty fees—some up to twelve thousand dollars—towards courses that promised job placement, often without results. "In a land of endless possibilities, one must tread carefully," they would warn, "not everything is as it seems."

Yet, Madhavi was a resilient woman who had seen this all and found her way through. An engineer by trade, she was keenly aware of the hurdles but had used her own grit to create stability and build a thriving career. She had established placement offices across four Canadian cities—a feat that wasn't achieved overnight. "Adaptation isn't just about learning the language or following the customs," she shared with me one day, "it's about genuinely rooting yourself in the soil of a place until it becomes a part of you."

Her family remained central to Madhavi. Her parents and brothers were back in India, and for years, she made annual trips home to reconnect, splitting her time equally between her parents and in-laws. But time brought its changes. Eventually, her parents and in-laws passed away, and she found herself growing distant from her Indian roots. A significant shift occurred when she observed her brothers' subtle withdrawal after their parents passed. Their demeanour changed as if fearing she might claim a share in the property, a common enough sentiment but one that stung deeply.

"Returning to your roots only to feel like a stranger is a strange, bittersweet sensation," she confided. These shifts led her to a new chapter in her life, one that involved adopting a daughter. She had seen her sister's and brother's children grow since birth, so she was determined to have a child. The idea of adopting a child perhaps would make her life meaningful and complete

She tried to adopt a child in Canada but failed. There were technical difficulties. The process itself was complex, with hurdles unique to cross-cultural adoption. Madhavi navigated Canadian adoption laws and chose to adopt a girl from an Indian orphanage, bringing her home and creating a new foundation for her life. Adopting a child was a different experience for Madhavi; she and her husband were happy after many years gradually both of them fell in love with that girl and got involved. Both of their lives had started to change for the better.

But life in Canada wasn't always easy. While Madhavi poured her love and energy into raising her daughter, there were always the whispers—strangers and even friends passing judgment. "Who knows what kind of child that is?" they would say, or "Will she be able to support you in old age?" Madhavi tried to brush these off, focusing on the love she shared with her daughter. Over time, her patience and strength won. The people around her slowly began to respect her choices.

In the professional world, however, the challenges were relentless. Madhavi's success in marketing led her to expand her company's clientele significantly. Yet, as the business grew, so did the company's demands.

Like many corporate tales, change came with a new CEO—Joseph. Joseph's primary mission, it seemed, was to reform and restructure, and he set his sights on Madhavi almost immediately. "A promise is only as valuable as its fulfilment," Joseph once said pointedly, criticizing her for making what he called "unrealistic assurances" to clients. He argued that her approach was a liability to the company's future, a viewpoint that was starkly different from that of her former management.

He brought his own team and strict demands for rigid schedules and traditional office culture, changes that weren't easy for Madhavi. Previously, she enjoyed flexibility in her work hours, balancing her demanding career with raising her adopted daughter, whom she had brought home. "Why judge me by clocking hours," she often mused, "when the results speak for themselves?"

However, Joseph was a stickler for routine and micromanagement. Biometric tracking was introduced, and all staff had to adhere strictly to nine-to-six work hours, with deductions for any deviations. Madhavi found herself struggling, trying to balance the new constraints with her personal responsibilities, feeling the weight of an unfamiliar, rigid structure that clashed with the results-driven culture she once thrived in. It became evident that this shift wasn't in her favour. Her salary was reduced, her motivation dampened, and a sense of discontent began to brew in her once-fulfilling workspace.

"I could bring in clients from anywhere, anytime," she argued with frustration, "Why not judge me by my targets rather than by a clock?" But her reasoning found no resonance with the management, and the decision had already been made. The new CEO and the owner paid no heed to her grievance around that time, such private placement companies were becoming very famous, and there was an economic boom because, in that decade, people were migrating from poor countries, and many government, semi-government and private companies needed skilled workers.

"Imagine creating the very thing that becomes your constraint," she lamented. Her frustration grew as she watched the CEO and other new recruits being offered sky-high salaries. She was the one bringing in clients, she reasoned, yet her role and rewards seemed to diminish. It felt unjust, a feeling that became a constant companion. What made it worse was that as a CEO, Joseph drew a salary of one and a half to two hundred thousand dollars a year. Madhavi, tried convincing that she had increased the company's business, by bringing in clients, and in return her commission and salary together she received was only seventy to eighty thousand dollars. According to her, this was unfair, and she questioned, 'Why this useless CEO is paid so much?' The company is running because of me, isn't it? Here they both had their first disagreement. The owner brought on a few more young marketing girls when the business was doing well, and Madhavi frequently clashed with them. "I am senior and who are these girls in front of me?" She began to feel that the owner and other staff were taking her for granted and was resentful. Gradually she went into depression.

We used to meet occasionally. I used to ask her about my job but realized that her own job was in jeopardy and she was getting very sensitive. We had a formal talk and discussions.

Despite Joseph's constant criticism, Madhavi's results had always been irrefutable. Her methods might have been unorthodox, but her impact on the company's growth was undeniable. The owner himself had long understood the effectiveness of Madhavi's strategies, yet he began to step back from openly supporting her, possibly due to pressure from Joseph. As monthly revenues continued to grow, the owner turned a blind eye to her contributions, prioritizing the company's bottom line over the personal impact on his employees. This left Madhavi isolated, deprived of both acknowledgment and support.

A fellow co-worker, a Canadian with a strong business acumen, had watched Madhavi's journey over the years and respected her unique approach and dedication and was well-acquainted with her remarkable work ethic. She proposed a partnership to Madhavi for new business.

Madhavi and she had both felt the shift in office dynamics under Joseph's leadership. This colleague, who had initially joined for career experience, now found herself equally disenchanted with the diminishing importance of individual contributions. Together, they began to see a new possibility—a joint venture where they could control their work environment and build a business on their own terms. "We can create something real, something that reflects our values," she proposed, inspiring a spark in Madhavi.

"Why don't we start our own venture?" the colleague proposed one day. "With our combined expertise, we could build a business that values true productivity and offers real support."

In the weeks that followed, they quietly laid the groundwork for their new business. After years of dedication and observing each other's strengths, they had a plan to start their own company. They conducted meetings outside the office, contacted potential clients, and ensured no one in their current company got a hint of their impending departure. When the time was right, they announced their resignations, finally stepping away from a place that no longer aligned with their values.

Her departure came as a shock to her previous employer. Despite their reluctance to see her go, they couldn't set aside their egos to retain her. The CEO, Joseph, assured the remaining staff, "Don't worry, I'll handle it." Yet, without Madhavi's deep understanding of the community and clients, the company began to falter. "Knowing the rhythm of your community is half the success in any business," Madhavi often said, a belief that guided her into her new venture.

Alongside her like-minded colleague, Madhavi registered their new business, pooling resources and knowledge to set up a small office. They worked tirelessly, building partnerships, fostering trust, and creating a network of reliable contacts. Madhavi was now committed to creating a transparent, client-centric business. She focused on ethical practices, ensuring her clients received authentic services and fair guidance—a stark contrast to the promises her previous employer often failed to fulfil.

As the business took off, Madhavi's network expanded rapidly, thanks to her ability to build genuine relationships. "A solid business is built on trust," she remarked. They soon established two offices and were able to serve a growing client base across multiple locations. Madhavi's emphasis on honesty and integrity in client relationships became the cornerstone of their success.

Now, Madhavi is a respected entrepreneur, and her company is known for its integrity and success. "Success feels complete when it touches lives meaningfully," she told me, reflecting on how far she'd come. Her daughter was thriving in college, her partner's career blossomed, and her supportive business partner stood by her side. Madhavi received several prestigious awards as a top entrepreneur, and organizations began inviting her to share her journey as a speaker.

Witnessing Madhavi's growth reminded me that, in Canada or anywhere, resilience, community, and integrity can lead to success beyond the typical corporate trajectory.

This tale of resilience, ambition, and friendship highlighted a common lesson for those of us pursuing careers in foreign lands: 'growth isn't always linear, and sometimes, stepping away is the best way forward.' The experience reaffirmed that we must often create our own paths, even in places as dynamic and resource-rich as Canada.

Morals vs. Million

Chapter Seven

Morals vs. Million

In Canada, my hopes were high, and my plan seemed straightforward: secure a job in my professional field, apply my skills, and continue life much as I had back home. But reality soon unravelled the simplicity of that dream. Despite holding professional degrees and years of experience, I quickly discovered that foreign credentials often carried little weight with Canadian employers. As I connected with fellow immigrants from India—engineers, doctors, and accountants who had left behind thriving careers to start afresh—I realized my struggles were part of a much larger narrative.

"Starting from scratch" is a phrase that takes on a new gravity for immigrants. It became clear that moving to a new country often demands more than just physical relocation; it asks for a complete reset of professional and personal identities. Even for those with coveted Permanent Resident (PR) status, securing employment in their chosen fields was far from guaranteed. While PR offered the legal right to live and work in Canada, it didn't promise the acceptance of qualifications or immediate access to opportunities. Each province, with its own unique rules and labor market dynamics, presented varying degrees of opportunity and challenge, making the job search feel like a labyrinth.

Over time, I encountered many who had arrived with similar aspirations, only to find themselves disillusioned. Some returned to India within six to eight months, having realized that the promise of a better future came with an unexpected cost. For them, the cultural shift toward a do-it-yourself mentality, the perceived lack of warmth in daily interactions, and the grueling pace of adaptation were too much to endure. Their bodies and minds, conditioned by years of stability and familiarity, resisted the relentless demands of starting over.

Canada, for all its opportunities, posed a formidable test of resilience. It was not just a matter of finding work but of finding oneself in an entirely new context—a challenge that not everyone was prepared for. This stark reality, I learned, was the unspoken price many paid for the dream of a new beginning. When I first arrived in Canada, I had high hopes. My plan was simple: find a job in my professional field, put my skills to good use, and continue life as I had back home.

Back in India, I held a respected job, and I was used to a certain professional status. Yet, within just a few weeks in Canada, the illusion that my qualifications would be enough dissolved. I was faced with "an inner struggle between the comfort of past achievements and the daunting path ahead in a foreign land." Adjusting to this new reality was far from easy, and like many newcomers, I struggled. At one point, I met people who had been in Canada longer, and some openly questioned my frustrations, saying, "Why should your journey be any easier than ours was?" It was humbling, but I also knew I would have to navigate this path on my own.

For the newcomers to Canada, I sincerely advice you: "Don't wait for the perfect job to come along; take what you can get, and focus on building your foundation." It is only by working alongside locals, learning their ways, and absorbing the local culture that you truly start to understand how to succeed. Looking back, I wish I had understood this from the beginning.

When I reached out to community centers and employment counsellors, I was directed to courses and workshops meant to "prepare" me for the Canadian workforce. It was helpful in some ways, but it also highlighted an uncomfortable reality: my skills and experience felt undervalued, and I had to invest in re-establishing myself. "Change, as I learned, was not just external but deeply internal, and without resilience, progress was unlikely."

In Canada, I observed that private colleges and placement agencies had become thriving businesses, especially for those willing to pay for opportunities to upskill. They catered to individuals like me who were eager to bridge the gap between where we had come from and where we aspired to be. Moving to a new country and pursuing success meant building anew, one step at a time. Canada, with all its complexities, taught me that flexibility and resilience are sometimes the most valuable skills you can bring.

During my early days in Canada, navigating my way through a new culture and job market, I met Deepesh Patel at a community gathering. Deepesh was a man in his early fifties, with a medium build, around six feet tall, often dressed in his signature safari suit. His face was always lit with a warm smile, yet his eyes hinted at a constant stream of thoughts. Even when seated, his feet moved restlessly, a sign of his boundless energy.

Deepesh, originally from a small town in Gujarat, was introduced to me as a successful entrepreneur in Canada, a man who had overcome countless obstacles. I was told, "In Canada, he's made a name for himself. He's someone who could show you the ropes." Desperate to establish myself, I felt ready to explore any opportunity that came my way. He learned that I held an MBA in Human Resources, and soon enough, he suggested that I assist one of his friends who ran a college in HR management. For me, it was my first real opportunity, a way to break into the Canadian job market.

As we spoke, Deepesh shared his entrepreneurial journey in Canada. A trained computer engineer, he was raised in a family of teachers who instilled discipline and a strong work ethic in him. After completing his engineering studies in Mumbai, he initially worked a corporate job, but the routine didn't appeal to him. He toyed with the idea of starting a business, but as he told me, "When there's no business background at home, convincing family about entrepreneurship is like asking for the moon."

After several failed attempts to find the right fit for himself, he set his sights on Canada, securing a visa to move there. Arriving with a dream and limited resources, Deepesh faced the daunting reality that his skills, though valuable, needed a fresh approach to stand out in this new land.

In Canada, he quickly recognized a gap in digital literacy. Personal computers were still new to many, and people were eager to learn. He thought, "If I can empower others with technology skills, I'll not only earn a living but also make an impact." This insight became the foundation of his business. With no capital to rent a proper facility, he began his computer training sessions at his own home, buying a second-hand computer from a local store. Setting affordable fees, he slowly attracted people who wanted to learn.

Word spread about Deepesh's courses, and soon he gained enough traction to move into a rented space. He formed partnerships with software companies, offering certified courses that drew even more students. His modest training center turned into a well-regarded institute, and he expanded to a larger facility to accommodate the growing demand.

Deepesh's journey was deeply rooted in the values he had inherited from his family in Gujarat, though he was the first in his family to venture into business. As someone adept at managing the ups and downs of business, Deepesh knew well how to make "one into two and then four," as he often said with a knowing smile.

After arriving in Canada, Deepesh had married Seema, a woman chosen by his parents back in India. Seema, with her Bachelor's degree in Commerce, was skilled in accounting and brought a sense of organization and structure to Deepesh's ventures. Though quiet in demeanour, Seema was diligent and financially astute, managing all the business finances and decisions. Whenever someone asked Deepesh about money or a business deal, he'd always raise his hands and respond, "Oh, you'll have to ask Seema about that," or "She's made the decision; I can't say otherwise." Together, they were a perfect team, with a shared understanding that allowed them to plan each step at their dining table the night before.

Building on their shared goals, Deepesh expanded his training programs, offering courses in essential software like Microsoft Word, Excel, PowerPoint, and Access. Soon, advanced modules in Word and Excel followed, attracting more students and steadily increasing his business footprint. Deepesh eventually invested in a prime spot in Toronto, purchasing an entire floor to accommodate his growing student body and the newly added IT courses. He even began collaborating with companies, providing them with trained employees who had skills in demand.

Through a contact, Deepesh learned about government grants available for skill-building courses. Canada's government was eager to support individuals who wanted to develop job-ready skills. As he explained to me, "The government funds training programs to ensure people have employable skills—good manpower benefits everyone." The educational institutions received these grants directly, while students attending these programs were provided a monthly stipend of $800 for up to eleven months to help with living expenses, though they were not expected to repay this amount.

With his growing reputation, Deepesh connected with skilled professionals from diverse academic backgrounds who had relocated to Canada. He carefully designed programs using their expertise and submitted his plans to the government for approval and licensing. Hiring a marketing team, Deepesh launched his college, which quickly gained traction, opening branches beyond Toronto. His institution's academic standards were not so commendable, but his unique approach of employing well-qualified, low-paid immigrant teachers made the college's reputation soar.

Though some questioned his use of underpaid talent, Deepesh saw it as an efficient business move. "If I can save on staff, I can invest in growth," he remarked, driven by a desire to quickly establish his financial success in Canada. His strategy was clear and unapologetic, blending opportunity with a bit of calculated risk, and for Deepesh, it paid off.

During this time, Deepesh proudly drove a high-end Canadian sedan Mercedes Benz, and his collection of cars and technical gadgets was something he took immense pride in. Despite his Patel surname, he was the first true businessman in his family. As I'd heard, back in the day, America had practically given visa exemptions to people with the Patel surname, because so many had ventured there, helping each other settle. Whether it was true or just a tale, only he could confirm, but one thing was certain—Deepesh had established his roots firmly in Canada.

With the growth of his business and college, Deepesh aspired to expand even further. He wanted to appoint a campus director and other senior staff members, just like the major colleges had, transforming his private college into a full-fledged university. Many advised him against it, saying he already had a solid, successful business and didn't need to take on extra risk. But Deepesh's confidence grew as he became convinced he'd cracked the formula for this business and could expand with four additional campuses. He was sure it was achievable.

To realize his vision, he began hiring professional staff, starting with a well-paid CEO, a foreigner named Stephen, who took charge and managed the college's operations. Stephen's expertise and network were a strong addition, and he quickly brought in additional staff to support the college. However, the fundamentals of Deepesh's college were shaky. With a focus on quick profits, he struggled to align with the educational standards expected in Canada, and within a year, his ambitious expansion plans began to crumble. Costs grew, revenue dwindled, and the college faced increasing challenges.

The college's pitch to students was simple but potentially problematic. Students were enticed to enrol with the promise of an $800 monthly stipend for basic expenses, claiming, "You'll get paid while you study!" Deepesh's marketing style had its risks, as Stephen, the CEO, warned. "This approach will raise red flags," Stephen told him. "If anyone reports us to the authorities, we'll face heavy fines." But Deepesh, unfazed, would respond, "Who's going to complain when everyone is getting what they want? People are happy—they're getting their expenses covered."

Yet, a different concern was brewing. Deepesh had hired Stephen, a senior, experienced CEO, who now understood the questionable aspects of the business. Firing him wasn't an option, as it would risk exposure of the business's vulnerabilities.

To keep him on, Deepesh kept Stephen and his handpicked team intact, even though it was financially burdensome. However, the strain began to show. Student enrolments numbers dropped from 250 to 200, and eventually to just 100 within a year. As a result, the college faced severe financial setbacks, and paying the expanded staff became a challenge.

Finally, Deepesh had to make a tough decision. He reduced the staff from 50 to just 20, trimming expenses where possible, but the scars of that expansion lingered, teaching him that not all ventures benefit from rapid growth without stability.

By then, Deepesh had realized that his student count had dwindled dramatically—from over 300 to just around 100. His decision to hire high-level executives had come at a high financial cost; salaries alone were bleeding over a hundred thousand dollars annually.

Firing the sales team was an option, but he feared it would further hinder student recruitment. For months, Deepesh had believed that bringing in a new CEO and extra investment would grow his college, perhaps even transform it into a university. But the reality had taken a harsh turn, far from his dreams of expansion.

"What once felt like a thriving business," he shared with me, "turned into an anchor pulling everything down." The very people who had been his allies started to distance themselves. Some important colleagues began to leave, tarnishing the reputation of the college. Operating costs became unsustainable, and he had to start selling off his college campuses and programs to other private colleges.

Despite the setbacks, Deepesh found a silver lining in his real estate holdings in Toronto. Property values had soared, yielding returns five to eight times higher than his original investment. Surprisingly, the sale of his college buildings brought in as much profit as the college business itself. With these funds, Deepesh bought a grand banquet hall, envisioning it as a venue for weddings, family gatherings, and corporate events.

Positioned in a prime area, the hall attracted constant bookings, and his investment in a quality catering service quickly turned it into a profitable venture. In just one year, he expanded, buying a second banquet hall and even a resort-like property in another city. "Compared to the college, this business quadrupled my returns," he would say with pride.

Deepesh's interest in the college waned as he dedicated himself entirely to this new line of business. He wound down all but one campus, strategically keeping it running because its courses held a valuable license that he planned to maintain until the right buyer came along. Twenty years had passed since Deepesh arrived in Canada. His children were grown, educated, and established in their own careers. At 65, he still spoke with an energetic curiosity about new business ideas. Money came in plentifully, yet one thing continued to elude him: social respect and the validation of a successful entrepreneur in the eyes of his community.

"Money I have, yes, but respect?" he would often say, a glimmer of disappointment in his eyes. Meanwhile, his wife Seema, thrived in her own world. She managed the finances with ease, finding joy in balancing accounts and watching over their children's lives. She found satisfaction in a life well-provided for, where wealth brought a sense of security and contentment. Yet for Deepesh, that elusive social acclaim was a persistent ache, one that Seema seemed blissfully unaware of.

Life is a Game!

Chapter Eight

Life is a Game!

I first met Anthony Thomas in October 2013, when I was still navigating my early months in Canada. After six months, a job continued to elude me despite my postgraduate degrees. Post graduate education in social service and management was at the core of my job. One day, in a local community center, where a counsellor recommended a certification program in social work from Ryerson University. It was an eight-month bridging course, essential if I wanted a job in Canada's social work field. Deciding to give it a shot, I visited the university's bustling downtown Toronto campus and enrolled in their initial communication module.

Classes began the following week, and as expected, the course was filled with middle-aged immigrants from various backgrounds, each eager to start a career in Canada. Friendships formed quickly in this group, united by shared experiences and dreams. Among them was Anthony Thomas, who soon became a close friend. At around 50 years old, Anthony was a towering figure, standing over six and a half feet tall, with a broad, heavyset frame and a receding hairline. His penetrating gaze missed little, giving him a thoughtful, almost inquisitive look. Having earned an MSW from an Indian university, Anthony was well-educated. Seated next to one another in the first class, we quickly became friends. Since we lived in the same part of town and shared the same subway and bus routes, our daily hour-long commute became a ritual of endless conversations.

Anthony and his family had come to Canada the same year as I did. In fact, he had managed the entire family's PR application process on his own, handling his, his wife's, his children's, and even his in-laws' forms. After securing permanent residency for all, he sent his wife and children to Canada while he stayed back in Gujarat, working as an HR Manager at a factory. With many years of experience in HR, he had a well-paying job with good perks. Born and raised in Gujarat, he was deeply connected to his roots. He completed his education in India, including his MSW, and it was during his studies that he met his future wife, also a social work student. Their love blossomed, leading to marriage and a joyful life with their two children—a boy and a girl.

Anthony's wife later pursued a B.Ed. and secured a teaching position in a local school, which provided a stable lifestyle. "Life was perfect back home," he often said, reminiscing about the fulfilling and joyous routine they had. Anthony's sister-in-law had also married those time, a marriage that was well accepted by the family. Both families lived side-by-side in close-knit harmony, their lives intertwined with shared stories and memories.

As political and social conditions in India shifted, Anthony felt increasingly unsettled. He began to feel a sense of insecurity in his own town, noting the changing dynamics and their impact on society. Anthony was outspoken by nature, unafraid to voice his political views, which, over time, had led to disagreements at work and even strained personal relationships. This open expression of his opinions often put him at odds with colleagues, and the tension began to impact his peace of mind.

As the social atmosphere in some parts of India became more polarized that time, Anthony's concerns only grew. His family, sister in laws family and close friends were very concerned. Anthony couldn't shake off his worries about their safety. Eventually, he came to the painful conclusion that he might need to uproot his family and leave his job for a safer future abroad. Canada seemed like a place where he could start afresh, free from the pressures and uncertainties of his home town. He had done his research thoroughly - Canada was known for welcoming immigrants, and job opportunities were available even for those of his age.

Anthony prepared meticulously. He filled out immigration forms not just for himself, but for his wife, his children, and his brother-in-law's family, ensuring they could all make the move together. Soon enough, everyone received permanent residency visas. When I met Anthony at Ryerson University's campus, I couldn't help but wonder what had brought him here, a man in his fifties with a partially bald head and a noticeably stout figure. His transition story, when I heard it, was nothing short of remarkable, and it made my own struggles to find a job feel almost trivial.

A dedicated learner, Anthony had seamlessly integrated into the university's social work bridging program. In contrast, I had left the program after the first course when I landed a full-time job that aligned with my HR degree. Supporting a household while navigating the costs of rent, travel, and daily expenses had made steady work my priority. For Anthony, however, education remained essential. He completed another course at Ryerson, which included Canadian experience and fieldwork components, embracing the learning process with determination. He read widely and expressed himself eloquently, making his return to academics after twenty years seem effortless.

"Learning is lifelong," he often remarked, showing a resilience I hadn't yet developed. Looking back, I can see now how Anthony was right, but it took me time to realize the value of his perspective.

For the first two years, however, Anthony struggled. His body was no longer accustomed to physical labour, and he found himself depending on the money he had brought from India. His wife found a part-time job at a school, which brought in a small income, but it wasn't easy.

During that period, I met Anthony often. I also got to know his wife and kids through various encounters. While he was immersed in his social work course, his wife often voiced her frustrations, especially about how their life had turned out after moving to Canada. "Why did we leave India to come here?" she would say, expressing the strain of their situation. "Back home, we were fine, and now we're here, and I don't even have a job." The frustration in her voice was unmistakable. She often remarked how odd it felt to see Anthony, who was once so full of confidence, slipping into bouts of depression. Most evenings, he would return home only to lay on the bed, eyes fixed on the TV, lost in thought.

Canada had a unique expectation of social workers—they needed to handle complex cases involving homelessness, addiction, mental health, and youth services. Anthony's wife imagined that educated people here led comfortable lives and pursued careers with stability and safety. But the reality hit hard: social workers often dealt with high-risk individuals and environments, and the job required a $100,000 insurance policy for personal safety. Moreover, workers were expected to have their own vehicles since public transport couldn't cover the entire commute. These hidden costs were eye-opening, but Anthony took it in stride. He completed the course, equipped himself with a solid understanding of the system, and secured a job in social work soon after.

In contrast, many participants had left the program midway, frustrated by the demands, but Anthony stuck with it. Those who left found it challenging to enter the field, as they hadn't qualified without finishing the program. He landed not just one but two jobs: one full-time during the day and another part-time in the evening. The urgency to work wasn't just for financial stability—it was deeply personal. Anthony was in his fifties, with diabetes and thyroid issues. He knew he was working against time and wanted to build a secure future for his family.

Anthony's wife also took on a part-time teaching position, although she wasn't thrilled about it. "MSW in hand, yet here I am in a job far below my capabilities," she'd sigh, a hint of resignation in her tone. While she had high qualifications, her priority was on supporting her children's education and overseeing their future. Though their kids were grown, her attention remained on them, ensuring their success and well-being.

Despite the health struggles, the long hours, and the steep challenges of adapting to a new country, Anthony was determined. Within a year of securing his job, he purchased a home for his family, a remarkable achievement gained though the circumstances were odd / challenging. This milestone brought a sense of pride, a visible reminder of the resilience he had built through perseverance.

When Anthony and his family moved to Canada, his children were in their mid-teens—his daughter was 17, and his son was 15. Arriving in Toronto, a sprawling, vibrant metropolis, was a big shift from their small town in India. Anthony's daughter adjusted as best as she could, diving into college and eventually landing a job, but his son struggled to find his footing. Adapting to a new culture, especially at such an impressionable age, wasn't easy. He tried school for a while but ultimately dropped out, unable to engage with either the education system or the expectations around him.

Anthony worked tirelessly, often taking on full-time shifts during the day and night-time stints at an education center. He knew what was at stake. "I don't have the luxury to stop. My family's stability is tied to these hours," he would say, with a weary but determined look. This relentless schedule became routine for him, especially as his wife decided to leave her job once his own position stabilized and they managed to buy a house and a car. She thought they could now take a step back and enjoy life, especially since their daughter had found a stable job and married a fellow Indian. However, for Anthony, the work was far from over.

His son, on the other hand, showed little interest in work or study. Now 28, he hadn't pursued any consistent job or career path. Handsome and charming, he was popular among his friends and often brought different girl-friends home, his relationships changing almost weekly. "He seems to enjoy the attention and the excitement of his social life," Anthony reflected one day. However, the father inside him worried, recognizing that his son's lack of direction could lead to an uncertain future. Anthony had come to Canada to give his children a better life, but watching his son's aimlessness left him feeling deeply disappointed.

Over time, Anthony's life in Canada grew more stable. He had a home, a car, and his daughter was settled. Still, there was a bittersweet undercurrent. "I may have achieved stability, but my son… I feel I have lost something irreplaceable in his journey," he confided. This pain was his silent burden, the cost of leaving behind a familiar life in India.

As time went by, Anthony often thought of his homeland, recalling friends and the comfort of familiarity. He frequently entertained thoughts of returning to India one day. "Someday, I'll go back," he'd say, unwaveringly. But he knew that so much of his life had now taken root in Canada. It was as if he was tied to two worlds, each pulling in opposite directions, a tension that seemed destined to remain with him forever.

The Silent Struggle

Chapter Nine

The Silent Struggle

Near our home in Mississauga City in Canada, there was a community center that offered various professional training courses, including ones on Engineering and HR. I decided to enroll in the HR bridging program as I thought I might find a job in human resources, especially as getting into social work here was challenging. The course was four months long. Coincidentally, an Engineering bridging course was also running at the same time, and it was there I met Rajiv Patkar.

Rajiv was a striking figure, somewhere between 35 and 40 years old, tall and well-built, with a charming presence. He had moved to Canada with his family just three or four months earlier. His wife, who had worked in banking in India, quickly found a position in a bank here, and within a month, they were set with a stable income. Having a secure job opened up other doors, like a favourable bank loan, so they decided to buy a house rather than renting.

During my time in Canada, the interest rate was remarkably low at just 1.8%, making home ownership an enticing prospect compared to renting. However, the decision to buy or rent is far from straightforward and depends on individual circumstances, financial readiness, and long-term aspirations.

Owning a home offers several advantages, the most significant being the opportunity to build equity over time. It also provides a sense of permanence and security that renting often lacks. For those planning to settle in Canada for the long haul, purchasing a home can be a strategic investment, shielding them from the unpredictability of rising rental costs. Additionally, homeowners enjoy the freedom to customize their living space—whether it's renovating to suit their tastes or adding personal touches— privileges often restricted in rented properties.

Ultimately, the choice between renting and buying comes down to priorities. While renting offers flexibility and lower upfront costs, ownership represents stability, growth, and the chance to truly make a house feel like home. Rajiv had a young daughter, around five or six years old, and since his wife was working, the responsibility of caring for their daughter primarily fell on him. While she was at school in the mornings, he would attend the training program, which ran early in the day. But once she returned home by 2 p.m., Rajiv would shift his focus to looking after her, leaving little time for a job search.

After the sessions, it became a routine for Rajiv and me to head for coffee. Those hours were filled with conversations about our lives, families, and the challenges we faced adapting to life in Canada. We became so used to each other's company that if one of us missed a day, the other would call to check in. As those three months passed, our morning meetings became a cherished ritual. In our talks, we would share not only our daily joys but also our concerns, forming a camaraderie that lightened the weight of adapting to a new country.

Rajiv was born in Mumbai at a place called Girgaon. He lived with his mother and younger brother, as his father had passed away when Rajiv was very young. The responsibility of raising the children fell entirely on his mother. Despite the hardships, both children were intelligent and did well in their studies, so their mother worked tirelessly to ensure that they had a bright future. She had a degree and had worked hard to secure a job in a corporate office in Mumbai.

Life in Mumbai was demanding. She juggled the household chores, packed lunches for her children, helped with homework, and cooked dinner, all while working 8 to 9 hours a day. Rajiv, being the elder son, excelled in school. He scored well in his 10th grade exams and pursued a science stream in high school. He continued to do well in his studies, completing his 12th grade with top marks, and eventually went on to pursue mechanical engineering at one of the renowned engineering colleges in Mumbai. His younger brother, on the other hand, struggled with his studies.

Rajiv's mother's hard work had paid off. The family's financial situation improved. They were able to afford a better life. Their small, modest house in Girgaon was a rented room under the "Pagdi" system—a traditional form of tenancy common in some parts of India, where tenants pay a nominal rent to the landlord for long-term residence. Although the house was not in the family's name, it became their home.

While the Pagdi system allowed tenants to live in a house indefinitely, it didn't offer the right to own or sell the property. The house was rented at an extremely low rate, but there were challenges in terms of maintenance and eventual eviction. Living in such conditions meant that buying a house would require significant financial investment, which the family had not yet saved for. With Rajiv's mother aging, they started contemplating buying a home, but the reality of how much it would cost, especially in Mumbai, was daunting.

Rajiv's mother knew the struggle of being away from home to secure a better future for her children, and yet, she also felt the pull of family tradition and responsibility. She had always worked hard to provide for her children and had sacrificed a lot to give them opportunities they never would have had otherwise. Now, it was time for Rajiv to take his next steps.

Rajiv had recently met Lily, a young woman from a Christian family from Goa, and gradually, their casual acquaintance developed into love. Lily was a pleasant, homely girl, but her background made the relationship more complicated. Rajiv's mother and brother were strongly opposed to the relationship. At the time, it was very shocking to see a young man considering marrying someone from a different religion, and his family was not comfortable with the idea. Even Rajiv's brother opposed the relationship, citing cultural and social differences.

Rajiv, however, was deeply in love and determined to marry Lily. He tried to convince his family, but they remained firm in their refusal. Eventually, after a lot of heartache and struggle, Rajiv made the difficult decision to marry Lily against his family's wishes. The path wasn't easy—especially given Lily's family's traditional values—but in the end, love prevailed. She was Marathi and from a good family, and Rajiv's family had no issues accepting her.

When Rajiv and Lily finally married, it was a bittersweet moment. Rajiv had always wanted to follow his heart, but doing so meant stepping away from the family expectations. In the end, despite their initial resistance, Rajiv's mother and brother accepted the marriage, though it was with mixed feelings. Rajiv had chosen to build his own future, and despite the challenges, the decision brought him both joy and sorrow.

Sometimes, the heart must make choices that the mind cannot fathom," Rajiv once told me over a cup of coffee, reflecting on his journey. It was a beautiful reminder that life in a new country, just like in love and family, requires navigating different paths, even when they seem difficult to walk.

Rajiv said "In India, we both were working in the same company, but according to company rules, Lily had to leave her job. However, due to her experience and education, she was able to secure a position at a large private bank". He mentioned that the job at the bank was a significant improvement and allowed the couple to dream of buying a house. But Rajiv's mother, despite the progress, was adamant that Lily would never be accepted in their home. Rajiv's mother would often scold Lily, making her feel uncomfortable with her presence. The constant bickering and the stress of their life in Mumbai led Rajiv and Lily to think about changing their living situation.

After much consideration, they decided to move to a new place where they could have some peace and space. Rajiv, who had grown up in a small house, found solace in the idea of moving away from the tensions of the old house. He felt that moving to a new place would help his wife find some peace and would also give him the opportunity to support his aging mother better.

Lily had a close friend in Canada, and it was through this connection that Rajiv and Lily decided to move abroad. They hoped that by starting fresh in a new country, they would find more opportunities and the chance to live a better life.

Rajiv, an engineer from Mumbai, left the familiar life in Maharashtra and moved with his wife to Canada. "Let's change the country; maybe we can change our lives," Rajiv said to Lily, a thought he carried with him as he left everything behind. It was a leap of faith, one that would shape their future in ways they couldn't yet imagine.

But the transition was far from easy. Rajiv had been unable to secure a job in his professional field, and so, he found work in the warehouse section of Amazon. From 9:00 AM to 1:00 PM, he worked at a logistics company, then worked in the warehouse from 8:00 PM until 1:00 AM. Despite his physical strength, the work was taxing. His job required him to work quickly and efficiently, and the wage was based on the number of packages he could pack in an hour. If he failed to meet the target, his salary would be reduced. "You can't afford to slow down," Rajiv remarked one evening as we sat together, sipping coffee. "Every minute counts, and it doesn't matter how tired you are."

Rajiv's physical work took a toll on him. He sometimes found himself exhausted to the point of illness. But despite these challenges, he was driven by the need to provide for his family and make the most of the opportunity they had in Canada. "I worked myself to the bone, but I couldn't give up," Rajiv said with a hint of pride. "We had no choice but to keep moving forward."

He spent long hours thinking of his family in Mumbai, especially his mother and younger brother. On the rare occasions when he took a break, he would reflect on the time he spent in Mumbai. "I would look at the pictures of Mumbai and remember how it felt to grow up there," Rajiv confided. "Sometimes, I missed the old days when we were together, but we knew this was for the best."

During his daughter's birthday, Rajiv invited me over to their new home, where we celebrated quietly, far from the noise of the past. As he looked at his daughter, he seemed to relive his own childhood, remembering his mother and brother. There was a heaviness in his heart as he thought of them. "Life is strange," Rajiv said softly. "We come so far, yet the past never really leaves us."

Rajiv would often speak nostalgically, his voice tinged with sadness. Sometimes, he would wipe his eyes secretly, unable to hold back the emotions. He would share memories from his childhood in Girgoan—his father, mother, brother, school, friends, home, the local market, the beach, and the games they played. It was evident that he missed those days. Though he was now able to buy a house and car, he couldn't take a single day off work. The financial situation was still tough. He often thought about the costs of traveling back to India, which could easily cost around four lakh rupees—a sum that was still out of reach.

Despite all their hard work in Canada, savings were minimal, and the dream of visiting India seemed distant. Rajiv had been doing his best to support his mother and brother from afar. His brother had recently married, but Rajiv had not been invited to the wedding, a source of ongoing resentment. Rajiv, however, had learned to accept that the rift with his family might never fully heal.

His daughter, on the other hand, was slowly adjusting to the new environment in Canada. Lily, his wife, had embraced the new world they were building, and the thought of owning their own house in Canada filled her with pride. "It feels good to have a place that's truly ours," she said. Their life in Canada was different from India, and they had come to terms with the fact that they no longer felt any strong attachment to returning. Rajiv's mother and brother had become distant figures in their lives, their relationship complicated by years of strain and distance.

There was a time when Rajiv had fallen ill, and I went to visit him. When I asked if he needed anything, he said, "I'm fine, just come by to chat, will you? I could use a little company." I took a bus to his place and found him weak, but still with enough strength to make tea for us. As we sat and talked, he shared his entire journey with me—his struggles with his family, his life in Canada, and how difficult it had been to reconcile the differences between his mother, wife, and brother. "For years, I couldn't choose between them," he admitted. "But now, I realize I've been torn in two for so long."

As time passed, Rajiv's mother became more and more entrenched in her views. She felt betrayed by Rajiv's decision to live in Canada and was reluctant to accept that her son had built a life without her. She could never come to terms with the fact that Rajiv was leading a separate life with his own family. His wife, Lily, and daughter had become his world, and despite the guilt he sometimes felt, he couldn't abandon the life he had started with them.

Rajiv's relationship with his mother and brother had always been strained, but it became even more complicated after his move to Canada. He would occasionally call his mother, but the conversations were tense. "Come see us sometime," she would say, but Rajiv knew that she would never leave her life in India to visit him. His mother was growing older, and Rajiv couldn't shake the feeling that he was failing to meet her expectations. "You can never fully escape the past," he told me once, his voice heavy with the weight of his emotions.

Despite these tensions, Rajiv never gave up on providing for his family. With Lily's job at the bank, their financial situation gradually improved. Rajiv had even managed to land a better job in his field as an engineer, and their quality of life improved. Slowly but steadily, they were able to buy a house and a car. "It was a hard-earned success," Rajiv said, with a hint of pride. "But there's always this feeling of emptiness, like something's missing."

Rajiv had made a trip to India alone not long ago, and during his visit, he stopped by to see his family—his mother, brother, and his brother's family in Girgaon. He noted how much the area had changed. The old rented house, which was once a symbol of his family's struggle, was now surrounded by new developments. "Things have changed, but it doesn't feel the same anymore," he remarked. "I can't help but feel disconnected from the place where I grew up."

His brother, who had settled in Mumbai, now had his own house in the suburbs, but Rajiv knew that his roots were still in Girgoan. His mother had always wanted him to return to India, but Rajiv had no intention of abandoning his life in Canada. "There are too many memories here," Rajiv said, his voice quiet. "I've tried to find a balance, but it's never easy."

Rajiv's life in Canada had changed in ways he never expected. Though his family was far away, he had created a life for himself and his family in a new land. He had found success in his career and stability in his personal life. But no matter how far he went, the feeling of longing for his roots in India, and the unresolved tensions with his family, would always remain.

As Rajiv continued to balance his past and present, he realized that while life in Canada had offered him new opportunities, the emotional distance from his mother and brother would never fully disappear. "I can't go back to the way things were, but I can't fully let go of them either," he confessed. "The pull of home is always there, no matter how far I've come."

In the end, Rajiv's journey was a reflection of the challenges many immigrants face—balancing the promise of a better life abroad with the pull of family, home, and the memories of what they left behind. His story is a testament to the sacrifices made in search of a brighter future, and the complexities of reconciling the past with the present.

Invisible Business

Chapter Ten

Invisible Business

While I was preparing the necessary documents and completing the paperwork for the visa application for Canada in 2011. It was an exciting yet daunting task. My application received a response in just five months, and to my surprise, my visa was approved. Initially, when I put my application for VISA, I had been told by my immigration consultant that it would take at least a year and a half to sometimes two years to receive a VISA or answer from the embassy. So, I had been mentally prepared for a longer wait. But suddenly, things were moving much faster than expected. The paperwork was complete, and within six months, I was expected to make the first trip with my family. Upon arrival, there would be more applications to complete, including receiving the permanent resident status.

As I started searching for people who could help me in this process. I began contacting everyone I knew. During this search, I managed to get the contact details of a director at a large social organization in Canada, including their email and phone number. His name was Mahesh Joshi. Mahesh had moved to Canada a few years ago and was now settled here. I contacted him through email and phone, but there was no response. I knew that Mahesh, who had worked as a director in India, must have a good position in Canada as well. I believed he could be of great help in securing a job for me. From my experience, people working in social welfare sectors are generally willing to help, often going out of their way to do so. Some even offer professional help, while others may go beyond their duty, just because they have the heart to assist.

I had no doubt that Mahesh, after settling in Canada, would understand the challenges of finding a job in a new country and would offer his support. Despite several attempts to reach him through calls, messages, and emails, there was still no response. I kept trying, hoping to connect with him, but nothing came of it. Eventually, I started crossing off names from my list of people who might help. The realization hit me: "This is your own personal battle, and you are the only one who can fight it." It became clear that, no matter how much I had tried, the journey to settle in Canada and find a job was ultimately going to be mine alone.

When I first arrived in Canada, I had no one left on my list who could help me. All the connections I had tried to make were either unresponsive or unavailable. My journey had shifted from waiting for external help to becoming fully self-reliant. I realized that I had to understand the local culture, adapt to the environment, and find my own path. The challenges were many, but as I learned more about the city and interacted with the people, it became apparent that the true value of my journey would come from embracing the new culture and integrating myself into the Canadian way of life.

As I navigated the complexities of adjusting to life in Canada, I reflected on the words I had heard so often: "This is your personal battle, and you must fight it." And indeed, it was. The long journey from uncertainty to eventual success was entirely mine to conquer. I learned to embrace the struggle, make connections where I could, and rely on my own abilities to carve out a life in this new world.

In the end, the journey wasn't just about securing a job or getting settled. It was about resilience, perseverance, and the realization that life in a new country brings its own set of challenges, but it also brings opportunities for growth, learning, and transformation. "Your future is shaped by your own hands," I told myself as I took each step forward, ready to face whatever came my way.

In the early days of my journey in Canada, my time was consumed with settling down—enrolling my son in school, setting up a bank account, arranging essential documents, and finding a home. About a month after our arrival, I received a call from Mahesh Joshi, a man I'd been trying to contact before moving. "I received all your messages and emails, but I was out of town and couldn't respond," he explained. To my surprise, he offered to meet and even drove over to pick up my family and me. Together, we drove to his home, which was in a neighbouring city. His house was a grand mansion, a rare sight to see for someone from our community in Canada. As I walked through the spacious rooms and admired the luxurious furnishings, I was impressed and thought, "This man must hold a prestigious position here; perhaps he can help me find my way."

We were greeted warmly by his family—his wife and two children. My wife and son accompanied Mrs Joshi another room while Mahesh and I went to his private lounge. Settling down, he gestured toward a glass cabinet filled with a collection of fine imported liquors and asked, "What would you like to drink?" I hesitated, but then he poured us both a glass of an expensive scotch. With a toast to new beginnings, we sat back as Mahesh began to share his journey.

"I worked as a director for a social service organization back in India," he began. "But I wanted to achieve something different, so I came here. The professional ladder has limits in India; there's an invisible ceiling in almost every office, and even in social work, there's a lobby for influential people who get selected for the top roles. I always dreamed of living abroad, and so I made the move."

He continued, "It took four years for me to secure a permit here. When I arrived, I started applying to various social work agencies and organizations, hoping my experience would land me a job in my field." But, despite a year of searching, he had no success. "Meanwhile," he admitted, "I took odd jobs at department stores, worked as a security guard—whatever I could do to bring in some income. I had two young children to care for, a wife who had always been accustomed to stability, and bills to pay."

Facing the financial pressure, he started exploring other ways to make a living. After talking with people in similar situations, he realized that there was demand in Canada for truck drivers and that the pay was good. "If you have a heavy-vehicle license and can drive a truck, transportation can be a profitable career," he explained. Since he enjoyed driving, he decided to go for it. He obtained his heavy-vehicle training and license, and through some friends he made in the field, he landed a job with a transport company.

In his words, "Sometimes, you have to step away from what you know and reinvent yourself completely."

This wasn't the career he had imagined, but it allowed him to support his family and build a stable life. As I listened, I began to understand the kind of resilience it takes to adapt to a new country and find a way forward, especially when things don't go as planned.

In Canada, I soon learned an unexpected truth: for an outsider / migrant, skilled trade jobs like masonry, plumbing, electrical work, haircutting, and repairs are highly valued and much better paid than managerial or administrative roles. Positions like "Manager" or "Director" don't necessarily pay well here, and administrative jobs often attract hundreds of applicants. But in the skilled trades, there might only be a few people in line for each job, making it far easier to find work. Over time, I found my way into the trucking industry and slowly learned every part of the trade. Among the drivers, I stood out as the most highly educated, and this earned me some recognition and higher responsibilities. Eventually, I was earning enough to buy a home, and my wife and kids were finally able to enjoy a comfortable life here.

The only drawback was that trucking involved long days on the road, with trips often taking four to five days before returning home. Trucks are equipped with modern amenities, including air conditioning, beds, and even autopilot for those long, open highways, which makes the journey comfortable enough. However, the nature of the work meant that I was often away from my family for extended periods, which made me feel disconnected. My wife and children were supportive, but I wanted to spend more time with them. Finally, after a year, I bought my own truck, hired a driver, and started taking on contracts independently. Bit by bit, I managed to grow, buying more trucks until I eventually had a fleet of four. Now, with more time and a good income, I'd achieved a level of stability I could have hardly imagined.

Listening to Mahesh's story was both fascinating and inspiring. He continued, saying, "Back in India, I was a director in a reputable social service organization. But now, I'm a truck driver in Canada." I could hear the honesty in his voice as he admitted, "How could I explain this to my friends back in India? I couldn't even tell you until now. But I thought, maybe it's better to be transparent once we meet in person." He smiled and added, "Just keep this between us for a while, alright?"

He reassured me that not finding work right away wasn't a sign of failure, saying, "Just because I struggled to find a job here doesn't mean you too will. We all have our own skies to reach for," he said with a laugh. "And from what I've seen of your experience, you might just find something. I can't say how, though."

I smiled and thanked him for his openness. "Knowing the reality of it is enough. I appreciate your honesty."

However, I admitted, "I can't even drive a car! I never learned back in Mumbai, and honestly, I don't have much interest in it."

Mahesh laughed. "Oh no! If you knew how to drive, I would have trained you on one of my trucks. But no worries, you can take driving lessons here and get your license. Once you're comfortable, go for the commercial license, and I'll help you however I can." Though I felt encouraged by his words, the idea of driving a truck made me a bit nervous.

The expensive Scotch I'd enjoyed earlier suddenly didn't seem to be helping anymore!

Our conversation shifted, and Mahesh gave me valuable insights into school systems, scholarship options, and other resources, which turned out to be quite helpful for my son. Through Mahesh, I realized that though the path might be daunting, Canada offered many possibilities if one was willing to adapt and try new things.

When I returned to India, some of Mahesh Joshi's old friends asked if I'd met him. I shared only that we had met in Canada, where he was now running a transport business. This, in truth, only scratched the surface of Mahesh's journey and success. Yet, his path posed a profound question: should he measure his current achievements in wealth alone, or in the financial security he had finally attained?

Back in India, Mahesh held a respected position as a social services director with an MSW, an MBA, and a wealth of experience. He had a certain standing in society, respect, and inner fulfilment. But, in Canada, he shared, the social work field lacks such respect, here, social workers who work closely with children, families, and the community are not always highly regarded, and they often face significant personal risks while working with clients like drug addicts, the homeless, the elderly, or AIDS patients. Because of these risks, Canadian social workers are encouraged to maintain personal insurance, own reliable transportation, and travel frequently for work—often on unpredictable schedules, which takes a toll on personal life.

Unlike India, where social work is viewed as a service to humanity, in Canada, it is strictly a professional role.

People from other countries are often hired for these roles because locals are less inclined to take on this high-risk, underappreciated work. For Mahesh, who had seen social work as a valued calling in India, the lack of social respect and prestige in Canada came as a shock.

When Mahesh first arrived in Canada, he attempted to find work in his field but quickly found that his Indian qualifications and experience didn't translate easily. Soon, he faced a challenging realization: the respect he had commanded in India was difficult to come by here. Despite his previous title and background, he now needed to start from scratch. However, his practical skills and willingness to adapt came to his rescue. Having always enjoyed driving, he eventually took up trucking. He completed his commercial licensing and started in the trucking industry, where his skill, education, and adaptability began to pay off. His life experience, ambition, and resourcefulness were ultimately what allowed him to thrive.

In time, Mahesh grew his business, acquiring ten trucks, hiring drivers, and setting up an office with dedicated staff. His business has reached new heights, turning over millions, and he is finally able to enjoy the security and success he once dreamed of. Now, when he visits India, he reconnects with family and friends, proudly sharing that he owns a transport business in Canada. He is generous with his Indian friends, donating to causes he once championed and supporting local social service organizations with regular contributions. He has become a successful entrepreneur recognized and respected by his friends and peers in India.

Perhaps one day, Mahesh might even receive a formal award for his achievements. But for now, his success—built on resilience, adaptability, and hard work—speaks for itself.

It's called Life!!!

Chapter Eleven

It's called Life!!!

While in Canada, I spent months tirelessly job-hunting. After nearly ten months, I finally landed a position as "Human Resources Director" at a college. Despite the fancy title, the pay was as low as they could offer. The college had around 40 staff members, a strong team, and was flourishing—but that success wasn't enough for the owner. Driven by his ambition to expand, he decided to double the staff and open new branches. This prompted him to hire an expensive new team, bringing in senior staff from other colleges for positions like CEO, Education Director, and Operations Director.

The intention, of course, was for the new team to help grow the business, but within six months, things took a downturn. The new management seemed more invested in making room for their own people than in improving the college, and they created a tense, unwelcoming environment for existing staff. People began to leave, either on their own or due to constant harassment. As HR, it fell to me to handle hiring and firing—and in one year alone, nearly twenty people left or were let go. Under the guise of "restructuring," the new management downgraded me from HR Director to HR Manager, keeping my salary the same but taking away authority. Within two years, my own enthusiasm had all but vanished, drained by the relentless turnover and the guilt of having to fire people who, like me, had come with dreams and hope.

Eventually, I left, too, without even having a backup plan. I applied for Canada's Employment Insurance (EI), a government program that provides temporary income support for those who have worked full-time for a minimum period and lost their job through no fault of their own. For four to six months, EI would provide 60% of my salary, and I was required to actively search for jobs and document my efforts. Leaving the country was also restricted during this period, as any absence could lead to the suspension of benefits.

The job search dragged on relentlessly. Each day was filled with networking events, countless meetings, and endless applications, yet the results were dishearteningly sparse. As weeks turned into three long months, a creeping sense of doubt began to overshadow my efforts. Though I still had a few months of Employment Insurance (EI) support remaining, the haunting question loomed large: *"What if nothing works out?"* The uncertainty gnawed at me, leaving me sleepless as my confidence ebbed away. Despite two years of effort and adaptation, I felt as though I had come full circle, staring at square one once again.

Desperation led me back to the Community Centers and Newcomer Centers I had turned to earlier. These spaces, staffed by counsellors who were often immigrants themselves, were meant to be a source of support. Yet, they offered a bittersweet refuge. While some staff members empathized with our struggles, others seemed preoccupied with their own survival. A few who had ascended to managerial roles appeared more focused on self-congratulation than fulfilling their purpose of helping others. Their indifference stung, leaving me feeling stripped of the little hope I had left.

Amid this turmoil, a job posting caught my attention—Sales Associate at a renowned luxury retail chain in Canada.

With over 100 locations and a reputation for excellence, the brand was familiar to many, and one of their branches was conveniently located near my home. Tentatively, I submitted my application. The process involved interviews and written assessments, each step fraught with anxiety. For the first time in what felt like an eternity, I was selected.

Relief washed over me, tempered by hesitation. While it wasn't the career path I had envisioned, it was a lifeline—a chance to rebuild and reclaim my confidence. Joining the team marked a new chapter, one that reminded me of the resilience required to keep moving forward, no matter how many setbacks the journey brings. My manager was a sharp, confident 25-year-old—a stark contrast to my own seasoned background. Reporting to someone significantly younger than me was a humbling, new experience. The first week was dedicated to on-the-job training, during which I learned about the intricacies of sales, completed in-house online courses, and got familiar with the art of selling domestic electronics. "Selling is not about convincing; it's about helping the customer find their solution," my manager once said, a mantra that stuck with me.

The store's dress code demanded impeccable grooming—suits, ties, polished shoes, and a constant smile. Initially, it felt suffocating to the formal attire daily. In my previous work, the only time I wore a suit and tie was at international conferences. Gradually, however, I adapted, observing others and embracing the change.

Yet, there was one area where I struggled—closing deals. My reserved nature and tendency to shy away from pushing customers often left me lagging behind my colleagues. While others were busy juggling multiple customers, I would sometimes spend hours with one indecisive buyer, only to see them walk away empty-handed. Despite this, I found satisfaction in the modest commissions I earned. While my colleagues raked in $4,000 to $8,000 monthly in bonuses, my earnings hovered around $1,800 to $2,200. It wasn't much, but it gave me a sense of achievement.

On the same day I joined, another new hire, Sajjad Khan, also began working at the store. A tall, well-groomed man in his mid-40s, Sajjad had recently moved to Canada. With a Master's degree in Political Science and a B.Ed., he spoke English, Urdu, Hindi, and Farsi fluently. His demeanour was polished, exuding an air of upper-middle-class sophistication.

We both attended the same training sessions, which helped us bond quickly. During breaks and lunch hours, we would chat about everything—from work challenges to life in Canada. As someone newer to the country, he would seek advice from me about settling in, while I shared my experiences and survival tips.

Sajjad Khan, originally from Asia, was a senior political journalist in his home country. He had worked with a prominent English daily and covered high-profile political and diplomatic events. Whenever an internationally significant figure visited his country, Sajjad was almost always on the guest list. His network of connections and the reputation he had built in journalistic circles gave him a certain level of influence and access to a privileged lifestyle. "It's not just about reporting; it's about understanding the pulse of power," he used to say.

However, the world of journalism wasn't devoid of politics itself. Like many journalists, Sajjad faced the challenge of climbing the ladder, which required not only skill but also political alliances. At a certain point, he realized he had to make compromises to sustain his position, and that didn't sit well with him. As the political and social environment in his country shifted, Sajjad began to worry about his future and, more importantly, the future of his children.

He decided it was time to seek stability elsewhere, to ensure a better life for his family. After years of observing global affairs as a political journalist, Sajjad concluded that Canada, with its structured immigration process and opportunities, was the ideal place to settle. "Canada seemed like a land of order amidst chaos," Sajjad later reflected.

With his wife, two young daughters aged 12 and 15, and an 8-year-old son, Sajjad took a bold step. He sold everything he owned in his country—his home, his land, and other assets—and moved to Canada permanently. He brought significant savings, enough to start a new life comfortably. His plan was straightforward: buy a house, get his kids enrolled in school, and find a way to re-establish his career in journalism.

Sajjad was optimistic about his connections with diplomats and foreign journalists, believing they could help him establish a foothold in Canada. Additionally, his children were immediately eligible for financial support from the Canadian government, receiving a monthly allowance of $300 to $400 each. This helped cover living expenses, while their schooling, was free until grade 12 that reduced further costs.

One piece of advice Sajjad received before his move turned out to be pivotal: "Take any job you can find initially. It will help you understand the local culture, improve your language skills, and give you Canadian work experience." This pragmatic suggestion shaped Sajjad's journey. Despite his background, he chose to start fresh by working at a local electronics store, selling domestic appliances.

To start a life in any new country, one needs to have some savings. Sajjad Khan, like most newcomers to Canada, rented a house initially to settle his family and enrol his children in school. He chose a neighbourhood close to people from his hometown for a sense of familiarity and support. An acquaintance from his village from his country advised him, "Buy a house here as soon as you can. It will give you stability faster."

In Canada, buying a house often proves more beneficial than renting. Rent for a small home ranged from $1,200 to $1,500, while the monthly mortgage for a similar or slightly bigger house was about $1,500 to $1,700. Additionally, owning a house came with an opportunity to earn through rentals. Renting out a room or the basement could fetch $500 a month, significantly offsetting mortgage payments. "Owning property here is like planting roots". This strategy, widely followed by immigrants, allows people to settle quickly while gradually building equity.

Sajjad started meeting new people, including some from his country community. While most were helpful, one acquaintance saw an opportunity to exploit Sajjad's trusting nature. One day, a known person approached him, claiming an urgent need for $50,000, which he promised to repay in two months. Sajjad, assuming the man's intentions were honest, handed over the cash without hesitation.

When the repayment deadline came, the man disappeared. His phone number was no longer active. Sajjad tried his best to locate him and finally confronted him after considerable effort. The man coolly denied borrowing any money, asking, "What proof do you have?" Sajjad realized he had no written agreement or receipt. His hard-earned savings were gone.

The incident taught Sajjad a hard lesson. "Frauds exist everywhere, no matter where you are," he reflected. It was a bitter experience, but it made him wiser about whom to trust.

Sajjad had initially dreamed of continuing his journalism career in Canada. But he soon discovered that Canadian journalism operated very differently from what he was used to in his country. In Canada, journalists often started with entry-level roles, and building a network required years of effort. For Sajjad, who had been a well-established political journalist back home, starting from scratch was daunting.

He began to feel disheartened. The savings he had brought were quickly depleting, and he couldn't find a role that matched his previous stature. "In my country, I was respected. Here, I'm struggling to explain who I am," Sajjad confided to a friend.

To regain some of his lost confidence, Sajjad started sharing old memories on social media. He posted pictures of himself with diplomats, celebrities, and political leaders he had worked with back in his country. On Facebook, he wrote, "Life may have brought me to a new land, but my experiences and connections are my treasures."

After moving to Canada, Sajjad Khan found himself holding on to his past identity as a prominent journalist. He started posting old photos on Facebook, showing himself alongside diplomats, political leaders, and celebrities.

It was his way of saying, "I'm still here, and I still matter." But the reality was different. His friends from back home commented initially, leaving remarks like "Good," or "Proud of you." Eventually, those comments dwindled.

"Post something new," a friend suggested. "Tell us what's happening now in Canada." That's when Sajjad realized he didn't have much to share. Life in Canada was a far cry from the prestige and recognition he enjoyed in his country. "The boat had already left," he thought to himself, reflecting on how disconnected he felt from his past and his new reality.

I met Sajjad while working part-time at a departmental store, where he worked full-time. His role involved selling furniture and electronics, a job that was target-based. He earned a base salary, but commissions depended on how much he sold. The store operated on a system where customers were assigned to salespeople in turn. When a customer entered, their number would be matched to a salesperson, who would assist them.

Sajjad excelled at this. His experience in journalism helped him connect with people and explain products convincingly. Customers felt comfortable around him. Meanwhile, I struggled. Many customers were just browsing (window shoppers), and they rarely made purchases. If a customer left without buying, they were called "no sales" customers (or burn leads). I seemed to attract more of these than anyone else.

One of our colleagues, a sharp and experienced Bengali salesman, was adept at spotting non-serious buyers. If he felt a customer was unlikely to purchase anything, he'd casually tell another colleague, "You go ahead; I need a break." This way, he avoided wasting his turn on non-buyers and kept his sales numbers high. Sajjad eventually picked up this strategy and started filtering out better opportunities.

While Sajjad was busy adjusting to his new job, his wife was focused on the family. Their two teenage daughters, aged 13 and 15, had grown up in a traditional environment back in his country. In Canada, they were suddenly exposed to a new, freer culture, which brought its own challenges. "How do we balance preserving our values while adapting to this new world?" Sajjad and his wife often wondered.

Recognizing the sensitive nature of this transition, Sajjad's wife decided not to work. She believed, "Someone needs to stay home and keep an eye on the girls during this crucial time." The youngest child, an eight-year-old boy, was less of a concern but still needed attention.

When Sajjad Khan first moved to Canada, his wife was thrilled about their new beginning. But her excitement faded as they settled into their routine. Soon, she began to feel the weight of their changed circumstances. They lived in a community with other immigrants, hoping to stay connected to their cultural roots. The neighbourhood women often gathered in the afternoons, gossiping about their lives and sharing grievances.

Hearing these stories day after day, Sajjad's wife started comparing their current life to their past. "What kind of life is this?" she would ask him. "You had such a good position back home, such respect. Now, look at where we are." Her constant remarks added to the strain on Sajjad, who was already struggling to adapt.

It didn't take long for Sajjad to realize that the problem wasn't just his wife's frustration—it was their surroundings. They decided to move to a different neighbourhood, away from the toxic environment. Gradually, the arguments subsided, and the focus shifted to building a new life. Sajjad learned an important lesson: "Support from your community can make or break your journey, but it's up to you to find the right people."

His struggles, however, were far from over. Even in the immigrant community, some people took advantage of him financially, which deepened his sense of isolation. His store manager, also from his country, gave him practical advice: "It doesn't matter who you were in your home country. Here, you need to build a new identity from scratch. Only then can you thrive."

Sajjad continued working at the departmental store, but he found little satisfaction. Sales targets, commissions, and dealing with uninterested customers made his job tiresome. Meanwhile, I had left the part-time role for a full-time job. Sajjad missed our friendly chats and found the work repetitive. Still, he stuck it out because the job provided some financial stability.

After some time, he switched to a bed-selling company and later moved to a second-hand car dealership. While the profits were better, he realized that constantly working against his values drained him emotionally. At home, support from his family was minimal, and the occasional sarcastic remarks only added to his frustration.

Despite these struggles, Sajjad worked tirelessly to expand his social circle. He started building connections with people who could help him grow. Through these contacts, he eventually acquired a gas station—known locally as a "petrol pump." This new venture offered him the opportunity to run a small general store alongside the station, creating additional income streams.

The station was located about 150 miles from Toronto, in a remote town along the highway. It meant being far from city life, but Sajjad didn't mind. Finally, he was making enough money to provide comfort for his family. His persistence paid off: he now owns a beautiful home with a garden and a car, and his children attend a good school.

Sajjad also became a respected member of the local community, even serving on the village council. He proudly told me over the phone, "Sir, you should come back to Canada. I'll help you get a gas station too!"

Sajjad's journey in Canada has been one of resilience and transformation. He now owns three gas stations, earning a stable income. Yet, the reason he left his homeland—to find a fulfilling, meaningful life—still eludes him.

Despite this, he has embraced his new life with acceptance and grace. As they say, "Time heals everything," and Sajjad has found a way to thrive in his circumstances. His story is a reminder that starting over is never easy, but with persistence and adaptability, it's possible to rebuild and find success.

"You may leave your past behind, but it always stays with you in some way," Sajjad often reflects. "What matters is how you use those lessons to shape your future."

Seeking Fortune, Finding Self

Chapter Twelve

Seeking Fortune, Finding Self

In my early days in Canada, I aimed to find work in social work or human resources management—fields I believed aligned with my experience and aspirations. Yet, despite my efforts, I found myself stuck, unable to make meaningful progress. The realization dawned that success in these areas required competencies I had yet to acquire.

Determined to find an alternative, I ventured into sales. However, this proved to be an ill-fitting choice. Convincing others, even for the simplest of products, felt like an insurmountable task. It was during one of these disheartening phases that a friend offered me some advice: *"Why not try banking? Even if you start with a temporary role, you could become permanent within a year. Banking jobs come with good pay and can provide the stability you're looking for."*

Encouraged by this suggestion, I reached out to a placement agency called People Connect and submitted my resume. My qualifications included only a basic graduate degree and some administrative experience in past—nothing extraordinary (I haven't mentioned about my two master's degree or the roles I have played). In Canada, I learned, resumes that overemphasize advanced education or senior roles can deter employers, especially for entry- or mid-level positions.

Understanding this, I adjusted my resume to fit the system. I highlighted essential qualifications, listed administrative skills, and avoided any mention of roles that might appear overqualified for the positions I was targeting. It felt strategic rather than dishonest—a necessary adaptation to navigate the job market.

Crafting a resume in Canada, or a *CV* (Curriculum Vitae) as it's commonly called, is a meticulous process. Unlike a simple record of education and past roles, a CV here is tailored to each job application, emphasizing how your skills and experience align with the job description. As one recruiter explained to me, *"In Canada, it's not about what you've accomplished in the past but how well you can present your potential to succeed in a specific role."*

This shift in perspective taught me the importance of adaptability and presentation in building a new career in an unfamiliar landscape. The lesson was clear: success in Canada isn't just about what you bring to the table; it's about how effectively you communicate your ability to meet the needs of the role. Placement services often charge anywhere between $100 and $500 to create a "winning resume." There's no guarantee of landing the job, but some agencies promise to at least get you shortlisted for interviews. Community organizations also provide free resume services. Many of their employees started out as immigrants themselves, making them more empathetic.

Interestingly, these community organizations function on a dual-purpose model. They genuinely help immigrants integrate, offering services like printing, computer access, and even legal support. However, these organizations are also under pressure to meet their monthly targets—helping as many newcomers as possible to justify government funding.

I discovered that people new to Canada often juggle assistance from multiple such organizations. It's not unusual for an immigrant to have their resume built or reviewed by three or four different agencies.

Despite their limitations, these centers serve an important purpose. They provide a sense of belonging for newcomers, a place to share struggles, find companionship, and occasionally, receive practical help. "Sometimes, it's not about getting the job but about feeling less alone while you search," said a staff member at one such center.

Crafting a resume, attending interviews, and learning to navigate the Canadian job market taught me some hard truths. It's not enough to just be skilled—you need to know how to package those skills in a way that fits the system.

Even though the process felt overwhelming and sometimes frustrating, these small steps helped me gain confidence. The community centers became my refuge during this time. They didn't just help me create resumes or improve my job applications—they gave me a reason to step out of the house, interact with others, and feel like I was moving forward.

Looking back, I realize that every challenge I faced in Canada was shaping me into a more resilient version of myself. As someone once told me, "The first job you get here might not be your dream job, but it's the first rung on the ladder. Don't stop climbing."

After tweaking my resume to match the Canadian job market's expectations, I finally got a positive response. The placement agency liked my simplified resume and called me in for online assessments. These included a test of my Excel, Word, and general analytical skills. To my relief, I passed and was offered a job as a bank clerk in a reputed Toronto bank.

The pay was decent—$18 to $20 per hour. The possibility of transitioning into a permanent role with a monthly salary of $30,000 to $35,000 was an exciting incentive. Without hesitation, I accepted the offer and joined the bank.

On my first day, I noticed that most of my colleagues were in their twenties. The team was filled with young, dynamic professionals between the ages of 22 and 30. There were only two of us who were over forty: myself and another colleague named Sushmitra, a soft-spoken middle-aged woman.

The work environment was modern and efficient. Everyone wore noise-cancelling headphones and focused intensely on their tasks, which primarily involved data entry. The atmosphere felt detached—no casual conversations, no bonding over shared work struggles. People were glued to their screens, utterly indifferent to the world around them.

Among this sea of silent workers, one person stood out—a vibrant young woman named Alka Gandhi. She was in her mid-twenties, with sharp features, a radiant smile, and wavy, shoulder-length hair. Alka had a lively presence and an energy that couldn't go unnoticed. She would always wear her headphones, occasionally humming loudly or chatting in bursts of excitement.

Her appearance and mannerisms made me think she might be Marathi, so I decided to strike up a conversation. I greeted her in Marathi, and to my surprise, she replied with a hesitant "Ho," before quickly switching to English. Then she announced, "No, no! I am Gujarati."

Her abrupt reaction puzzled me. Why would she deny any connection to Marathi so firmly? Curious, I decided to dig deeper, and over time, I came to know Alka's story.

Alka had grown up in Mumbai, in a predominantly Marathi neighbourhood called Parle. She had lived there her entire childhood, attending school and college in the area. Marathi culture surrounded her, and she had many Marathi friends.

In college, Alka met a boy who changed her life. He was handsome, charismatic, and they were in the same class. Their friendship grew naturally—they travelled to college together, worked on assignments, and spent endless hours talking. Eventually, this bond blossomed into love. His name was Mandar Karkhanis.

Alka's boyfriend came from a prominent Marathi family that owned a manufacturing business. His family was well-educated, cultured, and well-known in their community. Though Alka's family was Gujarati, they too were progressive and respected in the neighbourhood. Both families knew each other well, and the entire locality was eager to see Alka and Mandar wed/ looked forward that Alka and Mandar would tie a marriage bond.

Alka, deeply in love, embraced Marathi culture wholeheartedly. She learned the language fluently, adopted local customs, and even perfected the art of making traditional Marathi dishes. She was determined to blend seamlessly into her boyfriend's family and build her future with him. But life had other plans.

Alka and Mandar's relationship seemed perfect on the surface. They spent time watching movies, going for long walks, and attending each other's family gatherings. Both families had accepted their bond, and there was an air of inevitability about their marriage. But over the years, Alka began to sense a growing unease.

Mandar was a kind and soft-spoken man. He treated everyone with respect, had no bad habits, and loved playing sports and exploring new places. But he lacked one crucial thing—ambition. Alka, raised in a Gujarati family with a deep-rooted entrepreneurial spirit, couldn't ignore Mandar's complacency.

Mandar's parents were wealthy, and he was their only son. With no siblings to compete with and a sizable inheritance awaiting him, Mandar saw no need to carve his own path. He had completed his graduation but showed no interest in pursuing higher education or any professional aspirations.

Alka, in contrast, had always believed in creating her own identity. She had a deep desire to achieve something meaningful in life, regardless of her family's financial status. She hoped that with time, Mandar would change—that he would be inspired by her drive. But her efforts to motivate him proved futile.

As the days and months passed, Alka became increasingly frustrated. She even confided in Mandar's parents, hoping they might influence him. However, their response was disheartening.

"We've tried talking to him, but he's happy with his life. He's not doing anything wrong; he just doesn't see the need to do more," they explained.

Mandar's outlook was simple: "Why bother when life is already comfortable?" This attitude might have been logical to Mandar, but for Alka, it was suffocating. She could see no future where her ambitions and his apathy could coexist.

One day, a close friend suggested an idea that seemed like a glimmer of hope.

"Why don't you both apply for Canadian PR (permanent residency)? Moving to a new country, away from the comforts of home, might push Mandar to step up and take responsibility," her friend advised.

Alka found the idea appealing. She discussed it with Mandar and managed to convince him to give it a shot. Together, they approached an immigration agent, gathered all the necessary documents, and prepared for the IELTS English exam, a crucial step in the process.

But as the date for the test approached, Mandar's lack of interest resurfaced. On the day of the exam, he simply didn't show up.

Alka, however, persevered. She aced the exam, submitted her application, and soon received the much-awaited approval to move to Canada. By then, it was clear to her that Mandar wasn't going to change. Their paths, which had once seemed so aligned, were now irreversibly divergent.

Deciding to leave Mandar wasn't easy. Alka had invested years of love and hope into their relationship. But she realized that continuing to stay with him would mean compromising her dreams.

"Sometimes, you have to let go of someone not because you don't care, but because they don't care enough to change," Alka reflected.

Taking a deep breath, she packed her bags and set off for Canada, leaving behind a relationship that had once been her entire world.

Arriving in Canada, Alka felt a mix of fear and excitement. She was stepping into a completely new life, one where she would have to rely entirely on herself. But for the first time in years, she felt free.

Her story is a testament to the courage it takes to choose yourself and your dreams over comfort and familiarity. As she stood at the Toronto airport, ready to begin her journey, she thought to herself:

"Life is about taking risks, and sometimes the biggest risk is walking away from what's holding you back."

In that moment, Alka wasn't just starting a new chapter—she was writing an entirely new book.

When Alka decided to move to Canada, her reasons were deeply personal. She hoped that the distance and a fresh environment might inspire Mandar, her long-time partner, to reconsider his approach to life. But as fate would have it, things didn't go as planned.

Mandar's indifference persisted. Within a year of Alka's departure, he seemed to have forgotten about her completely. No calls, no messages—not even an attempt to reconnect. Alka was heartbroken.

"I thought love would inspire change. Instead, I found myself alone, carrying the weight of shattered expectations," she reflected.

Mandar's lack of effort to contact her left Alka devastated. She had hoped he might fight for their relationship, or at least that his parents would reach out. But there was nothing—only silence. For Alka, this silence spoke volumes.

"Sometimes, the hardest goodbyes are the ones where no words are spoken. You just feel the door quietly closing," she realized.

In time, Alka stopped expecting any form of reconciliation. The pain of rejection, however, lingered. Special occasions like festivals only amplified her sorrow. She found herself unable to enjoy traditional Marathi celebrations, as they reminded her of Mandar and the life she had left behind.

Over time, Alka's pain transformed into resentment—not just toward Mandar, but toward everything she associated with him. The warmth she once felt for Marathi culture began to cool.

"When love dies, it doesn't just leave a void—it sometimes plants seeds of bitterness," Alka thought.

She began to criticize the Marathi community openly. She compared them to other groups, particularly the Gujarati and other communities she had grown up admiring for their ambition and unity.

"Marathi people only know how to fight and argue," she would say. "They've done nothing to build Mumbai; it's the Gujaratis and others who made it what it is today."

Her once fond memories of her childhood among Marathi neighbours became clouded by her frustration. This growing disdain was a stark contrast to the pride she had once felt.

Years later, as she looked back on her journey, Alka began to see how deeply her heartbreak had shaped her perspective. Her anger toward Mandar had spilled over into her views on an entire community.

"It's strange how one person can influence how you see the world? But in the end, those feelings reflect your pain, not the truth," she admitted.

Canada became more than just a new home for Alka—it became a place of healing. She found herself surrounded by people from diverse backgrounds, each with their own stories of struggle and resilience.

"Sometimes, moving away isn't about running from the past—it's about finding the space to heal," Alka concluded.

Though her journey was marked by heartbreak, it also gave her the strength to rediscover herself. And as she moved forward, she learned that leaving bitterness behind was the first step toward embracing the life she truly wanted.

When Alka moved to Canada, she carried with her the burden of a broken relationship and the hope of starting over. But starting fresh is easier said than done, especially when unresolved emotions and deep-seated resentment shadow every step.

Her days were filled with work at the bank, where she excelled, yet her conversations often circled back to her past. One person in particular—Mandar, her ex-partner— remained at the forefront of her mind. The frustration with him had grown into a broader disdain for her own community.

One day, a colleague and friend at the bank, Samar, decided to confront her.

"Alka," he said firmly, "you say Marathi people are lazy and entitled. But, aren't we as immigrants doing the same, have we not taken the jobs that local people of Canada own. Imagine if they spoke about us the way you talk about your own community."

His words hit her hard. For the first time, she was forced to reflect on her bitterness.

Over time, Alka found a true friend in Samar. They began to share lunches and discuss life beyond work. Samar helped her see things differently, challenging her to focus on her growth rather than her anger.

"You can't rewrite your past, but you can decide how much of it controls your future," Samar would remind her.

Gradually, Alka started letting go of her resentment. Her perspective about her community began to shift as she realized that not everyone fits the mould of her painful memories.

Months turned into years, and Alka's hard work paid off. She earned a promotion at the bank, marking a turning point in her life. Feeling more grounded, she decided to take a break and visit India.

But instead of going to her parents' home in Mumbai, she went to Ahmedabad to stay with her uncle. There, she spent a month reconnecting with her Gujarati roots. This time allowed her to rethink what she wanted from life, and it led to an unexpected turn.

Through family introductions, she met a kind and ambitious man from her uncle's community. After getting to know him, she agreed to marry him. For the first time, she felt like she was making a choice not influenced by her past.

As Alka looked back on her journey, she understood the value of adapting not just to a new country but to a new mind-set.

Her story serves as a reminder that while new opportunities can transform your life, true change begins from within. For Alka, her journey to Canada wasn't just about building a career—it was about rediscovering herself and learning to let go of the weight she had carried for so long.

The Happiness Quest

Chapter Thirteen

The Happiness Quest

Life has moments when it feels like the world has come to a standstill. Progress halts, and everything around you seems frozen in time. Some people accept this phase with quiet resignation, others fight against it with all their might, while a few simply wait, hoping for change to come. But there are those who see this as a chance—a chance to rediscover themselves, break free from monotony, and start anew.

They say, *"Happiness is not a destination; it's a state of mind."* But what happens when even that state of mind feels out of reach? In such moments, the support of a friend who believes in you—especially when you've lost faith in yourself—can be a lifeline. I was fortunate to have such a friend during my time in Canada.

Let me introduce you to Baby Thomas, a man with an unconventional approach to life. He was restless by nature, never content with where he was or what he had achieved. Every job he took seemed like a stepping stone to something better, and within weeks, he would grow dissatisfied, yearning for more.

"The perfect job doesn't exist," he often said, yet he remained perpetually in pursuit of it. His restless energy and constant quest for improvement taught me a lot about the complexity of human ambition. While his journey seemed chaotic, it was also a reminder that dissatisfaction, when channelled wisely, can lead to growth and transformation.

My reasons for moving to Canada were deeply personal. My son's health and the desire for my family to be together were at the heart of this decision. Professionally, I had no reason to leave. I had spent 11 years in a rewarding job, progressing from a Program Officer to Director.

"It was the best job of my life," I still tell people.

This role allowed me to travel extensively across India and the world. I worked with an inspiring team, had the freedom to innovate, a supportive budget, and colleagues who were always ready to help. It was a dream job in every sense.

But life, as it often does, had other plans.

When I made up my mind to move to Canada, I thought of Baby Thomas. Originally from Kerala, he had settled in Canada and worked in the social services sector. He encouraged me to consider the country, assuring me that the transition wouldn't be too difficult and that finding a job would be manageable with his guidance.

His words were comforting. I imagined having him nearby, a friend to lean on during those initial, uncertain days.

Upon reaching Canada, I discovered that the reality was quite different. While I had chosen one city, Baby Thomas lived thousands of miles away in another. Traveling to meet him wasn't easy—public transport between our cities was sparse and prohibitively expensive.

The bus or train journey could take two or three days, and flights, though faster, were far too costly for someone starting fresh in a new country.

"Sometimes, life has a way of reminding you that not all plans work out," I thought.

While my decision to leave my rewarding career and come to Canada was difficult, it helped me grow in ways I hadn't anticipated.

"Life isn't about settling; it's about striving for the next big thing." These words perfectly capture Baby Thomas, a man who lived with relentless ambition and a restless heart. a towering presence, both literally and metaphorically. Baby Thomas was a charismatic personality, standing six feet tall with sharp features, bright eyes, and a confident demeanour that reminded me of South Indian actor Arvind Swamy. Born in Kerala, he moved to Maharashtra to train in social service, where his natural charm and intellect quickly caught everyone's attention.

After a brief stint in Mumbai, Baby Thomas landed a position as an administrator at a hospital in Pune. It wasn't just his qualifications—a double MS degree—that got him the job. A local bishop, impressed by Baby's abilities, recommended him for the role.

Once in Pune, Baby became popular among his colleagues, especially the female staff. His confidence and warm nature earned him admiration, and some were willing to go to great lengths for him. Despite the attention, Baby remained grounded and focused on his work.

During his time there, he met and married a Christian nurse from Kerala. It was an arranged marriage with blessings from both families. But as marriage brought new responsibilities, Baby began to feel constrained by his close ties with colleagues, fearing it could complicate his personal life. It wasn't long before he began searching for jobs in Mumbai, dreaming of bigger opportunities. "Sometimes, to grow, you have to leave comfort behind."

In Mumbai, Baby quickly found a job in the social service sector. However, his ambitions didn't stop there. He started applying for positions in the UK, a dream he nurtured even as he worked hard to support his growing family. His wife had also secured a stable job, and they welcomed their first child.

For Baby's wife, stability was key. She hoped to see her husband settle in one place. But Baby's habit of changing jobs often led to tension between them. He was a "Saturday husband," as she called him, present only on weekends, with work dominating the rest of his time.

Despite the challenges, Baby's determination pushed him forward. Eventually, his efforts paid off—he received a job offer from Scotland, a part of Great Britain. For Baby, this was a dream come true.

"When ambition meets opportunity, the heart soars."

Arriving in Scotland, Baby was ecstatic. The culture, the people, and even the weather were a stark contrast to what he was used to in India. At first, the unfamiliar dialects and customs posed challenges.

"Every beginning is hard, but persistence makes it worth it."

Scotland wasn't just about a new job; it was about adapting to a different way of life. Over time, Baby found his footing. He learned to navigate the local culture and built connections in his workplace.

"The heart of a restless soul never finds comfort in settling down." This adage fits Baby Thomas perfectly. From the green shores of Kerala to the misty hills of Scotland and eventually to the vast plains of Canada, Baby's life was a series of moves, each driven by ambition and a yearning for more.

A year after moving to Scotland, Baby Thomas brought his wife and their daughter to join him. His daughter quickly adjusted, finding a school with ease. His wife, however, struggled to secure a job. Despite her qualifications, finding employment in a new country proved challenging.

During this period of uncertainty, their second child was born, further adding to the family's financial responsibilities. With two children to care for and his wife still jobless, the burden of running the household fell entirely on Baby Thomas. The strain started to show.

His wife, once a senior professional in India, found it difficult to adjust to her new reality. Frustration mounted, and she often blamed Baby for the upheaval in their lives. As tensions grew, so did their arguments. But Baby, though hurt, pressed on. After two years of searching and numerous attempts, his wife finally found a job at a hospital.

With both of them employed, the couple decided to buy a house in Scotland—a symbol of their roots in this new country. They worked with a reliable agent, found a suitable home, and started paying the mortgage. Over time, life began to stabilize. Their children were doing well in school, and Baby's wife found her footing in her job.

However, challenges persisted. One incident at his wife's workplace shook her confidence—a patient accused her of being overly rough during a treatment. Though the management investigated, the situation reeked of bias. Feeling unsupported and isolated, she began to lose interest in her role. Still, she persevered while quietly searching for better opportunities.

Eventually, her efforts paid off. She secured a better position with a higher salary at another hospital. With her earnings, she learned to drive, bought a car, and found new independence.

While his wife found new motivation, Baby Thomas began feeling restless again. His social media feed was filled with pictures of his friends in Canada, enjoying their seemingly perfect lives. The allure of Canada's opportunities and lifestyle rekindled his desire for a change.

Now armed with British citizenship, he saw an open door to explore another chapter. Without much hesitation, he applied for permanent residency (PR) in Canada. Two years later, he received approval.

This decision, however, was not welcomed by his wife. She had just started to feel settled in Scotland. They had a house, stable jobs, a good life, and children thriving in school. To her, moving yet again felt unnecessary and disruptive.

"Why uproot ourselves again when everything is finally stable?" she argued.

But Baby Thomas was determined. Once he made up his mind, there was no turning back.

Baby Thomas's journey in Canada was marked by new beginnings, unexpected challenges, and a relentless pursuit of stability. His life, much like the Canadian wilderness, was unpredictable but full of lessons.

Upon moving to Canada, Baby Thomas secured a job as a child welfare social worker. The position, however, was located in a remote village two hours away from the nearest city. The commute was arduous—just one bus in the morning and one in the evening connected the village to the outside world.

For his family, village life came with its own set of challenges. The basics—schools, stores, and essential services—were available, but not much else. Baby Thomas had only one car, which made life difficult for his wife, who often needed to visit libraries or community centers to search for a job. Without public transport or another vehicle, her mobility was severely restricted.

Amidst the struggle, the family welcomed a third child. Baby Thomas was overjoyed at every addition to the family, celebrating each birth with immense pride. However, his wife bore the brunt of raising three children in a new country. With no support system, her career aspirations were often side-lined.

As their eldest daughter grew older, she began to help around the house, but the workload was still overwhelming.

Tensions escalated between Baby and his wife. She accused him of prioritizing his career over their family's well-being. He, in turn, argued, "I am the one working to support all of us. Why can't you find a way to manage both work and the kids?"

Their disagreements grew frequent, fuelled by the stress of their circumstances.

Feeling stifled by village life and longing for urban opportunities, Baby Thomas began searching for a job in Toronto. His experience of over a decade in social work helped him secure a role in a city 200 miles away. Though it wasn't Toronto, it was significantly closer to urban comforts compared to the remote village.

With cautious optimism, the family packed up and moved again. This time, Baby Thomas was determined to create a better future for himself and his family.

The new city offered better opportunities but was not without its challenges. In smaller towns and cities in Canada, invisible barriers like subtle racism often hinder integration. Locals were sometimes hesitant to accept outsiders, especially immigrants.

Despite these difficulties, Baby Thomas adapted and found his footing in his new role. But even here, stability was elusive. Over three years, he faced two layoffs due to budget cuts. Each time, he managed to find a new job, a testament to his resilience and skills.

Baby Thomas's wife had been ambitious, aspiring to join the medical sector in Canada. She attempted the qualifying exams three times, but failed each time. According to the country's rules, failing the test thrice permanently disqualified her from working in that field. This shattered her dreams.

Determined not to give up, she shifted her focus to caregiving and completed a home care course. Though she found work, it wasn't lucrative, with limited income from personal clients. Frustrated but resolute, she decided to enrol in a nursing course—a full-time, three-year program. At 44, going back to college was no easy task, especially with three children and household responsibilities.

Her days were a whirlwind of lectures, assignments, and caring for the family. Stress began to take a toll, and arguments with Baby Thomas became frequent. Tensions escalated, with a couple of incidents even leading to physical altercations. She filed a police complaint against him, and their families intervened to mediate.

Amidst their personal turmoil, financial pressures loomed large. The house they had bought in Scotland was now worth less than what they owed on it. Despite paying the mortgage, the value of the property had halved. Similarly, land investments in Kerala weren't yielding any returns.

Debt piled up like uninvited guests who refused to leave. "When you carry the weight of dreams on your shoulders, the climb feels steeper with every step."

After completing her nursing course, Baby Thomas's wife secured a job. For the first time in eight years, she was working full-time and earning a stable income. Together, they began chipping away at their debts and eventually bought a house in Canada. The mortgage for the new house added to their expenses, but it was a step forward.

Their children had grown up witnessing their parents' constant arguments. While they were close to both, they often sided with their father during disputes. Now teenagers, they would occasionally ask their parents, "How did you manage to stay together all these years despite fighting so much?"

Baby Thomas would laugh off the questions, unwilling to delve into the emotional scars beneath his light-hearted demeanour. But inside, he knew that their relationship had been strained for years. The burden of constant sacrifices—financial, emotional, and personal—had left them both tired.

At 53, Baby Thomas still wasn't content. Despite years of hard work, a family, and a home, he felt unfulfilled. He had started a public administration course, hoping to land a government job.

Even now, he was chasing something—though what exactly, even he wasn't sure. "Am I searching for success, stability, or just a sense of purpose?" he often wondered.

His wife, though equally tired, kept striving. Her perseverance gave him some solace, yet he couldn't shake the feeling of emptiness. Looking back on 25 years of marriage, he reflected, "I have everything I ever wanted, yet it feels like nothing at all."

Baby Thomas's journey is a reminder that sometimes, life is less about reaching the destination and more about understanding why we started the journey in the first place. His story remains open-ended—a tale of endless pursuit, resilience, and the unrelenting human desire for something more.

For those walking similar paths, his story is both a caution and an inspiration: "If we don't recognize what we truly seek, even the greatest achievements can feel hollow."

The Turning Point

Chapter Fourteen

The Turning Point

"Sometimes, you need to step away to truly understand where you belong."

Between April 2013 and October 2016, I lived in Canada, trying to settle down and build a life. I gave everything I had—taking up odd jobs and trying to make ends meet. Yet, something inside me couldn't adjust to the rhythm of that life.

Throughout these years, I visited India three times during my vacations each trip back felt like a tug at my heartstrings. I saw a rapidly changing India—socially, economically, and in terms of opportunities. My friends and family seemed to be thriving, and I couldn't help but feel drawn back to my roots.

My son had also reached an age where he was becoming more independent. His schooling in Canada was coming to an end, and he was preparing for university. I realized he didn't need my constant presence as much anymore.

By April 2016, when I returned to India for a break, I had already made up my mind. I would return permanently. "There's something about home—it doesn't just call you back, it anchors your soul."

In October 2016, I packed up my life in Canada and decided to move back. It wasn't an easy decision, but it felt right. Canada, for all its beauty and opportunities, had shown me that settling there wasn't in my destiny.

Coincidentally, just as I had decided to leave, a great job offer came my way in Toronto. It was stable, with a promising career path and a better salary. For a moment, I hesitated. Was I making the right choice?

On the other hand, I had already accepted a job offer in Mumbai in my own professional field. Backing out felt wrong, as I had given my word. Moreover, my wife wasn't keen on staying in Canada anymore, and her support meant everything to me.

"Sometimes, it's not just about what you leave behind, but about who you're moving forward with."

We initially moved to Canada with the hope of spending more time together as a family. Back in Mumbai, I had been so consumed by work, long commutes, and commitments to social causes that I rarely had time for my wife and son. The hectic pace of life had led to small but growing tensions in our family. We thought moving to Canada would provide a slower, more peaceful life where we could focus on each other.

But life in Canada didn't turn out as expected. While the healthcare and schooling for our son were excellent, other reasons for our move didn't materialize. Financial pressures, cultural adjustments, and the lack of familiar support systems made settling down harder than we imagined.

By October 2016, my decision to return was firm. I was fortunate to land a job in my sector in Mumbai because of my earlier connections in India. The organisation had agreed to an online interview, and when they offered me the position, I felt like I had been given a lifeline.

Back in India, I looked forward to reconnecting with my profession, my friends, and my extended family. I was excited to contribute to my field again and felt ready to embrace the opportunities India had to offer.

"Goodbyes are never easy, especially when they are final."

During my stay in Canada, life threw challenges that I never anticipated. Five close family members back home in India passed away during those four years. I lost my uncle, aunt, two elder brothers, and a sister—all people I cherished deeply. Having already lost my parents in my youth, these losses were devastating.

Being so far away during their last moments was heart-breaking. I couldn't say a proper goodbye or be there to offer my support. This weighed heavily on my heart, leaving me questioning my decision to move to Canada. No matter how hard I tried, settling down in Canada seemed elusive, and this grief only deepened the sense of failure I felt.

On the day of my departure from Toronto, my 17-year-old son accompanied me to Pearson International Airport. We took the bus together, a simple yet significant journey from home to the airport. He was in his 12th grade at the time, with just eight months remaining until his final exams. My wife had planned to join him in 20 days to provide company and support as he prepared for this crucial phase.

Leaving him alone for those weeks was a source of anxiety for me. It was the first time he would be on his own in a foreign land. Yet, his calm demeanour and confidence reassured me. "Sometimes, our children surprise us with their resilience, reminding us of the strength we've instilled in them."

Over the years, my son had become more than just my child—he was my closest companion. From the age of 11 to 17, he had matured into a responsible young man, taking on small family duties with remarkable ease. In him, I found not only an ideal son but also a trusted friend, someone who stood by me during life's ups and downs.

My flight on October 18th was with British Airways, taking me back to India via London. The journey, spanning 21 hours with a layover, gave me ample time to reflect. As I waited to board, I noticed many others like me—travellers heading home to India. October and November often see a wave of people returning to escape Canada's unforgiving winter. With temperatures plunging as low as -20 or -30 degrees Celsius, life becomes challenging, especially for those without personal vehicles. For many, these flights are a gateway to the warmth of family, a break from the cold, and a return to familiar comforts.

As I hugged my son goodbye, I carried with me a mix of pride and longing—pride in his readiness to face challenges and longing for the days when he was still my little boy. Life in a new country teaches us many lessons, but saying goodbye to loved ones, even temporarily, never becomes easier.

Once aboard, I settled into my seat near the tail-end of the plane. It was a window seat on the left side of a row configured with two seats on either side and four in the middle. Next to me, in the aisle seat, sat a woman who appeared to be in her mid-40s, though I'm terrible at guessing ages. She was dressed in a corporate-style outfit—shirt, pants, blazer, and tie—suggesting she might be on an official trip.

As we made eye contact, she smiled, and I returned the gesture. Breaking the ice, she asked, "Are you headed to Delhi or Mumbai?"

I replied, "Mumbai. What about you?"

She smiled and said, "Punjab via Delhi."

That meant we would travel together until London, where we'd change flights. It felt comforting to share this leg of the journey with someone, even if we were strangers.

After a while, my fellow passenger and I began conversing again. This time, I asked her if she was returning home after finishing a business trip. She smiled softly and clarified that while this wasn't a business trip, she had been living in Toronto, Canada, for many years. She was now traveling back to her own home in India. Her name was Simran.

She showed a genuine interest in my story, and I was waiting for an opportunity to unburden my thoughts. I shared with her my journey in Canada so far, the challenges I faced, my experiences with people there, and how I had finally made up my mind to return to Mumbai for good.

Simran listened attentively, nodding at times, and then said something that struck a chord: "At least you've made the decision to return. Many people don't even have that option."

Her words resonated deeply. Over the years, I had seen many immigrants in Canada who remained stuck in limbo. For various reasons, they couldn't return to their home country. They had severed the ties that might have allowed them to go back. As a result, they adapted to the local culture and lifestyle, but often with a sense of resignation rather than joy.

Gradually, Simran began sharing her own story. We delved into topics like culture, values, and the emotional connections we hold with our roots. She revealed that she was headed to Punjab, to her ancestral home (she mentioned the name of her village, but it escapes me now).

She said she made it a point to visit her village at least once a year, usually for a month. The reason was more than nostalgia; it was a matter of necessity. Simran loved her village, and the timing of her trip coincided with the pleasant season. But she also made these trips to reconnect with relatives and ensure her family's land and property remained secure.

"It's not just a visit; it's about protecting what's ours," she explained. Every year, she reviewed all the necessary documents, cleared any pending dues like property taxes and utility bills, and ensured that everything, from their fields to their home, was safe.

I was astonished. "Really? You mean you have to visit every year just to ensure your property is safe?"

Simran gave me a knowing smile. "You may find it hard to believe, but it's the truth. You might have heard or even experienced that many people lose their lands, houses, or businesses back in their home country after moving abroad."

She went on to explain that local villagers, fuelled by envy towards those who had settled abroad, often took advantage of the situation. With the help of corrupt local officials, they would claim the property as their own or create false ownership records. Some would even go as far as filing fake police complaints or trapping families in fabricated legal cases to prevent them from traveling back to their home countries.

"It's heart-breaking," she said. "And once someone is caught in this web, their path back home is blocked. They can't even fight back properly because they're not physically present. Sometimes passports or PR cards are stolen or withheld, making it impossible for them to return or even leave the country they are in."

As Simran shared her experiences, I found myself drawing parallels to my own village in Konkan. While I had heard of disputes and envy among villagers, I had never witnessed such extreme behaviour first-hand. Could it be that things had changed in the past decade? Or was this an issue more prominent in other regions?

Simran's story felt like a revelation—a reminder of the complex ties that bind immigrants to their homeland. "For some, home is a place you never leave behind, no matter how far you go," she said thoughtfully.

As I listened to her, I couldn't help but reflect on the emotional and practical challenges faced by those who straddle two worlds. For Simran, returning home every year wasn't just a sentimental journey; it was a necessity to protect her heritage. For me, going back to Mumbai felt like reclaiming a part of myself I had lost during my years in Canada.

Simran shared a story with me during our flight that left me speechless. She and her husband had settled in Canada 15 to 20 years ago. Her husband worked in a senior position in a corporate company, and Simran herself was employed at another corporate firm. In the beginning, they had worked extremely hard to establish themselves in Canada. They had struggled financially at first, but eventually, they earned well, had good luck, and managed to buy a nice house. They had also secured a car and other comforts.

Their family in Punjab was always supported, both financially and emotionally. Every year, they sent financial help for maintaining their farms and other family matters. They even sent money to buy more land in the village and to build a farmhouse. Simran's husband's younger brother, who was very close to them, managed the family's business and affairs back in Punjab. He even had the power of attorney to handle any property dealings.

Initially, due to their busy corporate lives and the struggle of settling in Canada, Simran and her husband couldn't visit their village for 8 to 10 years. However, despite the distance, they consistently sent money and ensured everything in their family's home was well taken care of. Their investments in both Canada and their native village were growing steadily, and once their children were old enough to go to school, they decided it was time to visit Punjab.

Simran, her husband, and their two children travelled to the village for two weeks. However, during this visit, Simran's husband, who was always engrossed in his business, found himself out of place in the village. He wasn't accustomed to the local customs, and despite staying there for two weeks, he didn't connect with anyone in the village. He didn't even know the people around him well.

"I could feel the distance in our own home," Simran confided. "In our own house, we were treated like guests, while my brother-in-law and his wife made all the decisions.

Even small things like decisions about household matters or daily activities required their approval." There was an overwhelming sense of unfamiliarity, a feeling of being outsiders in what was supposed to be their home.

After their visit to the village, they returned to Canada, and Simran couldn't stop thinking about the changes she had seen. She spoke to her husband about her observations, but he seemed uninterested. He was too absorbed in his regular routine to give much attention to the matter.

Simran then reached out to her friends and relatives in Punjab to gather more information. A few weeks later, she received shocking news. Her brother-in-law had illegally transferred land and property into his own name without any permission from Simran's husband or her family.

"I couldn't believe it," Simran said. "I felt so betrayed."

Simran immediately informed her husband, but his response was calm, almost indifferent. "I trust my brother," he said. "He's always been reliable, and he must have had a reason for doing this. Let it go, Simran. We're busy here, and we have more important things to focus on."

Simran was in disbelief. She decided to investigate further and went to the village herself to verify the information. When she spoke to the villagers, they reassured her that there was no issue. "Everything is fine. Don't worry. Some people are just trying to stir things up."

The villagers sent her all the necessary property documents, and everything seemed in order. However, when Simran shared this with her husband, he still refused to take the matter seriously. "People are just jealous of our progress," he said. "Don't make a big issue out of this. There's no need for panic."

Simran's husband was so convinced that everything was fine that he brushed off her concerns. Yet, Simran couldn't shake the feeling that something wasn't right. Her husband had blind faith in his brother, but Simran couldn't ignore the nagging sense of betrayal and mistrust.

Simran had been working in the corporate sector for years, and she had heard plenty of stories about illegal activities and corrupt practices in her home country. However, it was when she decided to visit India on her own that the truth started to unravel in ways she never expected.

She had spoken to her husband about it, and he had given his consent. So, Simran decided to travel back to India, to visit her family and see for herself what was happening. She arrived in Punjab and stayed with her friend, Hadar, whose family was living there. From the start, she could sense something was off. There was a bitterness in Hadar's conversations, and Simran felt like she needed to return to Canada sooner than planned.

After a couple of days, Simran decided to visit the local panchayat office and land records department to gather information about the property and land documents. But when she asked for the records, she was told that the people in charge were too busy, and that she would have to come back. Simran went back multiple times, each time being given a new excuse. Weeks went by without progress, and the situation became frustrating.

During her stay, Simran slowly began to build connections in the village. She spoke to neighbours and started learning more about what was happening with the property. To her shock, Simran heard that her brother-in-law had illegally taken over land and property that belonged to her family. Not only had he transferred the documents into his own name, but he had also bribed local officials to make the process smoother.

Simran realized that the situation was much worse than she had imagined. She had been paying for these land deals for years, but now it seemed like her brother-in-law had taken everything without permission.

"This is more than just a family disagreement," Simran thought to herself. "I've been robbed by the people I trust the most."

Determined to get to the truth, Simran went to the local police and court, hoping to find support. Fortunately, the authorities agreed to help, but soon after, her brother-in-law began pressuring Simran with threats. He used abusive language and even threatened to kill her.

"This is no longer just a family matter," Simran realized. "This is a dangerous game, and I'm in the middle of it."

The situation was becoming more intense by the day. Simran's brother-in-law had already taken millions of rupees worth of land, houses, and trees and even the ancestral property from her family. He had the power and the resources to do whatever he wanted without fear of consequences. Simran knew she had to act quickly before it was too late.

In the midst of all this, Simran confided in her husband, who was shocked by the news. He was completely unaware of the situation and agreed to help. Simran also arranged to stay at a nearby hotel for safety, while the local goons assigned by her husband's friends began to protect her. She stayed in a farmhouse she had purchased earlier, away from the village's eyes.

For nearly a month, Simran lived in isolation, with only the hired bodyguards for company. Some days, it felt like a nightmare. She couldn't sleep, always on edge, unsure of what might happen next. But as the days went by, Simran realized that the people assigned to protect her were not just goons—they were actually looking out for her safety, making sure she had everything she needed and were genuinely concerned about her well-being.

"In a strange way, they're protecting me more than my own family ever did," Simran reflected one night. "It's the most ironic thing I've ever felt."

Simran continued to fight the legal battle, determined to retrieve the property documents. Slowly, with the help of the local police and court officials, she was able to get the property back under her family's name. The documents were restored, and the land was returned to her rightful ownership.

The fight didn't end there, though. It took years for everything to settle, but Simran had won. The land, the house, the crops, and the trees that had been wrongfully taken were finally returned. Simran also hired a local family to manage the property and made regular visits to ensure everything was in order.

Every year, Simran visits the village in October to check on the property and make sure everything is running smoothly. She meets with the villagers, helps out where needed, and has built strong relationships with them over time.

"The struggle was hard, but it brought me closer to the people who truly care," Simran said one day. "I now know who has my back, and that's what really matters."

Simran's husband began to appreciate the importance of these visits. Although he still doesn't feel the need to stay in the village for long, he accompanies Simran for a week or so every year. He's begun to understand the deeper connections Simran has with the village and the people there.

But even though things have calmed down, there's still one question that lingers in Simarans husband mind: "Why did my brother do this? Why betray family for money?" Simran's husband continues to visit the old acquaintances in the village, taking small gifts as a way to show his goodwill.

Simran's experience taught her that no matter how far we go from home, the past has a way of catching up with us. Sometimes, the familiar faces we trust the most can turn out to be the ones who hurt us the most. But in the end, it's the strength to fight for what's right that truly matters. "Sometimes, we are forced to fight for the things we love, but it's in those battles that we discover who we really are."

Our conversation was flowing smoothly, but it wasn't until the pilot's announcement that we realized how much time had passed. Simran and I had been talking non-stop for almost 4 to 5 hours. In between, we had breakfast, lunch, and made trips to the restroom, but none of it interrupted our conversation. We were so engrossed in our discussion that time just flew by. Finally, the plane began its descent, and we were landing at our destination.

As we stepped out into the airport in London, Simran's next flight was connecting to Delhi, and I was heading to Mumbai. We exchanged warm goodbyes and wished each other the best for the journeys ahead.

Simran had shared a story with me that opened my eyes to many things. Hearing about her struggle for justice, I realized the immense strength she had in fighting against the people and systems she once trusted. She had fought for her rights and against injustice in a way that was truly inspiring. I was deeply moved by her courage and determination.

Walking into Toronto's bustling airport while returning, I felt the weight of my struggles and disappointments pressing heavily on my shoulders. The challenges I had faced, the setbacks, and the lingering uncertainty of my journey had taken their toll. But something shifted during my time in Canada. Conversations, encounters, and observations began to offer me a fresh perspective.

I realized that my pain, while real, was far from unique. Millions around the world were grappling with far greater hardships. The life I was living, with all its imperfections, was a dream for countless others. This thought stayed with me, reshaping my outlook:

"The life you are living is the dream of millions."

As I reflected on this, I began to understand the resilience of those around me. People facing monumental challenges were still finding ways to persevere. Their determination forced me to confront my own narrative. What excuse did I have to dwell on my struggles when others were conquering theirs with such fortitude?

My thoughts wandered to Simran's village, her battles, and the lives of the people I had encountered in Canada. Each story, each face carried its own burden. Some were fighting for survival, others for justice, and many were chasing elusive dreams. It struck me that every individual holds a story—an intricate tapestry of trials, triumphs, and lessons waiting to be uncovered.

I realized the importance of truly seeing people for who they are. Everyone has something valuable to share, but understanding their stories requires both empathy and an open heart. As I navigated Toronto's streets during my stay, I found myself paying closer attention. The diversity of lives and experiences around me became a source of inspiration, a reminder of the resilience of the human spirit.

"We must have the right eyes and a good heart to truly understand the stories around us."

My journey, which had begun as a personal quest for answers, evolved into something far greater—a journey of understanding. It became a window into the broader world, where each encounter held the potential to teach me something new. Life, I realized, is more than our individual struggles; it's a collective narrative of humanity, rich with untold stories.

This revelation brought me peace and a renewed sense of purpose. I began to appreciate the privilege of my own life and the opportunities it offered, even in moments of hardship.

Beyond Borders: My Travel Memoir

Chapter Fifteen

Beyond Borders: My Travel Memoir

"Every person is happy or sad for their own reasons. Sometimes we don't even realize what we want or what we've been seeking until we grow older."

We know this very well that people living in our country can be happy or sad but when people choose to move abroad in search of happiness, there is often a deeper quest involved. I've often wondered: what if people could find the happiness they were looking for when they moved abroad?

I remember reading a story in my childhood, "Beyond the Seven Seas, there was a city," which made foreign lands seem so alluring. The idea of living abroad held a fascination for many, and people have countless reasons for wanting to move to other countries. Some of these reasons make perfect sense, while others are more personal. But, over time, the difference between what one hopes to gain and what one actually experiences abroad becomes more apparent. Sometimes we adjust to these differences easily; at other times, it's harder than we expected.

In my own journey, I saw people who were already settled in India—successful businessmen and even families—who travelled abroad in search of greater success. But when faced with the challenge of adapting to a foreign culture, economy, and way of life, many of them had to return. Even highly educated professionals from prestigious institutes like Indian Institute of Technology (IIT), Indian Institute of

Management (IIM), or doctors and engineers found it hard to adjust to the new systems and ultimately came back to India. After returning, they would often say, "My country called me back," as a way of explaining their return, almost as if they had been on a mission and had fulfilled it.

"Success and failure have different meanings for everyone. For some, it's about finding their place in the world, while for others, it's about creating something bigger."

People have their own definitions of success, and sometimes, the path to that success involves multiple struggles. Some find the courage to return to their roots, even if they have to face the judgments of others. In India, when someone returns from abroad, they are often met with whispers of "failure" or "giving up." This social pressure sometimes discourages people from coming back, so they continue to fight to make a place for themselves in foreign lands, hoping that one day, success will validate their choices. While some succeed in this quest, the price they pay—emotionally, socially, and mentally—is often high.

In my observations, the people who thrive in foreign countries are those who manage to connect with the local culture, practices, and mind-set, or at least adapt to them while staying true to their roots. Successful Indians abroad have not only adjusted to foreign systems but have also contributed significantly to fields such as technology, business, medicine, and more.

"Success is not just about where you are, but how well you adapt to the place you've chosen."

Take for example the Indian-origin leaders in the global business world, such as Satya Nadella of Microsoft and

Sundar Pichai of Google. These individuals have reached the pinnacle of success by understanding not only their professional fields but also by understanding the cultures they were working in. This is a prime example of how connecting with both worlds—the old and the new—can lead to a powerful sense of accomplishment.

Similarly, many successful Indian entrepreneurs in Silicon Valley have made their mark and inspired countless others. These entrepreneurs and start up founders, who once came from India, have built global empires through innovation and a relentless drive to succeed. In the field of education and research, Indian scholars and scientists are known for their ground-breaking contributions worldwide. Indian doctors, too, have earned global recognition for their skills and dedication to healthcare.

"The world is connected, and those who can bridge the gap between cultures, countries, and traditions often achieve greatness."

In other sectors as well, Indian-origin individuals are making strides. They've succeeded in various fields such as literature, music, sports, and politics. Many Indian politicians have held prominent positions, representing their communities in foreign governments. Whether it's as ambassadors, senators, or ministers, these individuals contribute significantly to the political landscape of their adopted countries.

Moreover, Indian athletes have raised the flag of their adopted countries high in international competitions like the Olympics, proving their talent and making their mark in the global sports arena.

When I reflect on the success of Indians abroad, I realize that it is often the result of a strong educational foundation, a readiness to work hard, and the ability to adapt. The culture of focusing on education and professional work in India has deeply influenced the achievements of Indians in foreign countries. But the personal qualities—such as perseverance, resilience, and adaptability—play an equally important role in shaping their success.

In my travels, I've encountered people whose dreams and needs were very different from mine. The question that kept coming back to me was whether these dreams, once fulfilled, would bring them true happiness. This book is my attempt to understand and share the journey of individuals who, like me, find themselves struggling between their home country and their new life abroad.

"Sometimes, the greatest challenge is not the distance, but the feeling of being distant from everything you once knew."

For someone like me, who always needs to meet and talk to people, staying at home alone for long periods was never an option. I realized that while I was learning new things and meeting new people, there were aspects of my own culture that I missed deeply. In my quest to understand the balance between my life back home and my life in Canada, I learned a crucial lesson: keep the old and embrace the new.

It's a simple rule, but one that I often found difficult to follow. The question of what is truly important to me, what I value most, was something I could only answer for myself. My family might have had a different perspective on this, but I had to make my own decisions. Many Indians who settle abroad naturally feel a strong pull towards their homeland, and this emotional connection is something I could understand deeply.

"Homesickness is a natural feeling—it's the emotional reflection of missing family, friends, and familiar surroundings."

Living away from home is not just about adjusting to a new country; it's about reconnecting with your roots while making space for new experiences. Homesickness is real. The absence of family during festivals, the longing for traditional Indian food, or the simple joy of being surrounded by people who speak your language can feel overwhelming at times.

In Canada, I found myself yearning for those familiar sights and sounds of home. Whether it was the smell of Indian spices cooking or the laughter of friends gathering during festivals, these small things made me realize how deeply tied I was to my culture. And yet, the experiences I was gaining in this new land were also valuable.

I've experienced this first-hand at Indian events in Canada, where I'd attend Hindi and Marathi music programs, or watch Bollywood movies with fellow expats. The energy of the crowd, the excitement of hearing old songs like "Chithi Aai Hai" that brought tears to many eyes—it was a powerful reminder of the bonds that tie us to our homeland. "The heart always remembers what the mind forgets." The nostalgia and connection to home are something that can never fade, even in a foreign land.

"The challenge of adjusting to new customs and traditions is what shapes us and helps us grow."

Adjusting to the local culture and fitting in with the people around you can sometimes be challenging. The social norms, language barriers, and differences in public holidays all take some getting used to. I often found myself struggling to understand the way things worked in Canada—the pace of life, the social interactions, and even simple things like the way holidays are celebrated there

Being far from family and friends during important events like weddings or festivals can be emotionally taxing. But over time, I began to understand the importance of connecting with local communities. Slowly, I made new friends, formed bonds, and found a new sense of belonging in this new place.

"When you live in a foreign land, you're not just adjusting to the environment—you're building a second home."

One of the most powerful things I've learned during my time abroad is the importance of blending the old with the new. The food, the festivals, the way people communicate—while these might be different from what we're used to, they don't take away from who we are. Instead, they become part of us. In Canada, I have had to navigate both the Canadian way of life and my Indian roots, which sometimes felt like a balancing act.

And yes, I missed the simple pleasures of home—the taste of authentic Indian dishes, the spicy aroma of a homemade curry, or the laughter-filled chaos of an Indian festival. These little things, though, made me realize how much I cherish my culture. But over time, I also discovered that there is beauty in embracing new experiences. The world is getting smaller, and as we move towards a more globalized society, it's possible to preserve our traditions while also being part of the larger world.

"The world is a bridge, and we are all travellers passing through it. It's about finding our place in the journey."

Chapter Sixteen

Settling Beyond Borders

If you find a tone of disappointment in the stories of this book, let me clarify—I do know that life in Canada is full of opportunities, and it is possible to achieve your dreams here. My aim was always to show my son that pursuing one's career and making it successful is possible, even in a foreign land. Canada offers ample opportunities for immigrants to build a successful career. The Canadian government actively supports immigrants and values the contributions they make to society and its economy.

In life, sometimes the choices we avoid can cost us more than the risks we choose to take. This is the hidden price of inaction—the opportunities missed simply because we hesitated at the wrong time. It's not just about what we didn't do, but about the growth, the experiences, and the rewards that slipped away in the process.

When we hold back, whether due to fear, indecision, or doubt, important moments pass us by. Opportunities like making investments, learning something new, or taking on a new project often get postponed, keeping us stuck in place. Time, as we know, is the one thing we can't get back, and with each passing moment, the potential of what could have been slowly fades.

It could be something as simple as picking up a new skill, starting that book you've been thinking about, investing in your future, or deciding to take that big step and move abroad. When we wait too long, we risk losing the progress we could have made. Similarly, even businesses that delay adopting new strategies or technology can fall behind and lose their edge.

For me, deciding to go to Canada was a choice to avoid the cost of inaction. Even though my journey there didn't unfold as I had hoped, it was a decision I don't regret. The lessons I learned from that experience, the people I met, and the challenges I faced, all added to my growth in ways I hadn't anticipated. It wasn't about success or failure—it was about embracing the opportunity to move forward and learning along the way.

The cost of inaction may not always be obvious, but over time, it adds up. It's often reflected in regret—wishing we had acted when we had the chance. Remember, every action requires effort, but the cost of doing nothing is far greater. It holds us back from progress and from realizing what could have been. So, even if uncertainty lingers, it's the steps we take that move us ahead. However, I want to share something important here: building a career in a new country takes time and effort. The process of establishing yourself and making progress in your professional life may take longer than expected. It requires patience, persistence, and a proactive attitude. But if you approach the journey with the right mind-set, your chances of success in Canada increase significantly.

Through the stories in this book, I hope to offer various perspectives on life in a new country. Whether you're moving abroad for work or to build a better life, one thing is certain: success doesn't come overnight. It's about being willing to take risks, put in the hard work, and stay focused on your goal. Becoming a part of a new community and adapting to a different way of life is a process that requires patience. Opportunities are available, but you must actively seek them out and remain determined to overcome any obstacles.

"The key to success is not just finding opportunities, but having the courage to pursue them."

In my own experience, settling in Canada wasn't just about finding a job or securing a place to live—it was about understanding the culture, learning to navigate social systems, and connecting with people. These things take time, some days are tougher than others. "Patience is bitter, but its fruit is sweet."

The process of becoming a part of a new country is an ongoing journey. It's not about arriving; it's about how you settle in and make a home for yourself. You have to allow yourself the time to adjust and learn from your mistakes you accidently do, finding the right opportunities might not be easy, but the persistence to keep searching for them is what will set you apart.

The stories you read here represent different aspects and experiences of people who came to Canada with dreams of making a better life for themselves. Each individual had to face the challenges of starting over, but they all shared a willingness to work hard, to adapt, and to seize the opportunities they found.

This book doesn't seek to draw any grand conclusions or provide a definitive answer. Instead, it offers a glimpse into the lives of people who decided to take a leap of faith and start anew. It shows the reality of the journey and encourages others to be brave and take the steps needed to fulfil their dreams, no matter where they are.

So, as you read through these experiences, I encourage you to take away your own lessons. The choices you make and the actions you take will shape your journey, just as they have shaped mine. And most importantly, remember: stay patient, stay determined, and success will follow.

In the future, I believe that experiences like mine, the sense of nostalgia and longing for home, may become less common as the world continues to connect more. Technology is bringing people closer, and soon, there may not be the need for such intense feelings of homesickness as we have today. But for now, this experience has been a profound part of my journey.

In the end, living abroad teaches us that we carry our homeland within us, wherever we go. Our identity is shaped not just by the place where we were born, but by the places we choose to call home. And while the world is becoming increasingly connected, it is this journey—between the old and the new—that truly defines who we are.

After spending time abroad and interacting with so many people from different walks of life, I realized that success is not just about reaching a destination—it's about the journey itself and how we evolve along the way. Some people find their calling in their homeland, while others discover it in foreign lands. But, in the end, we all carry a part of our homeland with us, no matter where we go.

In my own journey, I learned that life is not only about pursuing happiness or success in one place—it's about learning from every place you go, and embracing what each culture has to offer. Every journey abroad teaches us something about who we are, and in the process, we build bridges between the world we know and the world we are learning to understand.

And through this understanding, we can truly say: "Success is not about where we are from, but where we are going."

About the Author

Mr. Shrinivas Sawant, has over 25 years of experience in working with not for profit sector both at local and international level.

Mr. Srinivas Sawant was born in a Kalsuli Village in Konkan, India came to Mumbai after 10th grade and did his graduation and post-graduation from Mumbai University. While in doing his graduation, he become member of National Service Scheme (N.S.S). Social service sector was introduced to him through NSS and then he got interested in that sector. Mr. Sawant then decided to do his career in social service. Mr. Sawant has done his Masters in Social work (MSW), Masters in Human Resource (MBA) and post graduate diploma in Project Management and Business Analysis.

Since 1990, he has been active in the field of social service and started working in the field of child welfare, supporting slum dwellers and slum community in Mumbai and in rural areas. He has extensive experience working with local, national and international organizations and donors.

Shrinivas moved to Toronto, Canada from April 2013 for good, despite having a strong experience in social sector and education in the field he has to struggle initially to meet his basic needs. While going through that struggle he made several friends there and understood there struggles simultaneously. He did not enjoy his journey at Canada and he decided to come back to India. And in October 2016 he returned to india and started his career again in social sector. The object of writing this book A Canadian Quilt – Stories of Immigrants is to capture the essence of the immigrant experience—dreams, struggles, achievements, and the emotional journey of individuals who set foot in Canada with aspirations for a better future.

Through 13 unique stories, along with the author's own journey, the book aims to showcase diverse immigrant experiences – Each story represents a different perspective, background, and aspiration, reflecting the challenges and triumphs of those who dared to dream beyond borders.

www.ingramcontent.com/pod-product-compliance
Lightning Source LLC
Chambersburg PA
CBHW060546160726
47991CB00001B/453